Healing after narcissistic abuse

Recover, Move on & heal yourself after a toxic abusive relationship with a narcissist. Recovering from emotional abuse & the effects of narcissism on a deeper level.

Jasmine Harriet

© Copyright 2018 - All rights reserved.

The content contained within this book may not be reproduced, duplicated or transmitted without direct written permission from the author or the publisher.

Under no circumstances will any blame or legal responsibility be held against the publisher, or author, for any damages, reparation, or monetary loss due to the information contained within this book. Either directly or indirectly.

Legal Notice:

This book is copyright protected. This book is only for personal use. You cannot amend, distribute, sell, use, quote or paraphrase any part, or the content within this book, without the consent of the author or publisher.

Disclaimer Notice:

Please note the information contained within this document is for educational and entertainment purposes only. All effort has been executed to present accurate, up to date, and reliable, complete information. No warranties of any kind are declared or implied. Readers acknowledge that the author is not engaging in the rendering of legal, financial, medical or professional advice. The content within this book has been derived from various sources. Please consult a licensed professional before attempting any techniques outlined in this book.

By reading this document, the reader agrees that under no circumstances is the author responsible for any losses, direct or indirect, which are incurred as a result of the use of information contained within this document, including, but not limited to, — errors, omissions, or inaccuracies.

Table Of Contents

Introduction
    Love.

Chapter 1 - Success Stories..........................13
Gabby, 3 Years Abused, Occupational Therapist

Wendy, 2 Years Abused, Travel Blogger

Laura, 5 Years Abused, Business Owner

You Can Recover

Chapter 2 - Victim Mode............................29

What Makes it Hard to Heal?
    A Disparity of Truth
    Clarity in Retrospect
    The Pit of Self Criticism
    Learned Powerlessness
    A Lonely Road
    Fear of the Unknown
    Laying Down the Facts
    Don't Expect Them to Change
    You Were Never the Problem
    You Shouldn't Feel Sorry for Him
    They Know What They're Doing

The Cornerstones of Healing
    Ask Why
    Be Specific
    Be Kind to Yourself
    Be Smart
    Stay on Top

Journal Writing Exercises

Chapter 3 - Getting Rid of the Pseudo Personality..45

Acknowledging Your Pseudo Personality

The Challenge of Dealing with a Pseudo Personality

Breaking the Machination
Stop Contradicting Yourself
Reflect on Your Behavior
Begin Self-Discovery

Chapter 4 - Inner Child Healing............................45

How Does it Happen?

The Inner Child in Adulthood

What Does a Stable Childhood Look Like?

Caring for Your Inner Child
Identifying Childhood Pain
Reparenting Your Inner Child
Engaging Your Inner Child

Chapter 5 - Creating Your Own Thoughts..............68

5 Steps to Regain Control
Get Rid of the Poor Self-Concept
Refocus Your Mind
Developing the Habit
Be Your Biggest Motivator
Keep Your Emergency Kit at the Ready

The Value of Mindfulness
Tips for Improving Mindfulness

How to Affirm Yourself

Chapter 6 - Survivor Mode..82

Is It PTSD?
How Can You Tell if You Have PTSD?

Getting Help

Gratitude Exercises

Chapter 7 - Thriving Mode...91

Building Self-Confidence
How to Re-Establish Confidence
Goal for Gold - Writing Exercises for Goal Setting

Chapter 8 - Getting into a New Relationship.........99

The Signs of Readiness

Redefining Sexy

Becoming Your Own Happiness

Single and Blessed

Conclusion..109

INDEX

Personal Recovery Journal

Day 1

Day 2

Day 3

Day 4

Day 5

Day 6

Day 7

Day 8

Day 9

Day 10

Day 11

Day 12

Day 13

Day 14

Day 15

Day 16

Day 17

Day 18

Day 19

Day 20

Day 21

Day 22

Day 23

Day 24

Day 25

Day 26

Day 27

Day 28

Day 29

Day 30

Other Exercises
   Journal Writing Exercises
   Begin Self-Discovery
   Engaging Your Inner Child
   How to Affirm Yourself
   Writing Exercises for Goal Setting
   Gratitude Exercises

Introduction

Love.

They say that it's one of the most powerful forces in the world. In a lot of ways, that can be true. Some of the greatest stories ever told were based on human experiences fueled by *love* - from the epic tales of ancient times, to contemporary million-dollar musicals that have taken over modern-day society. Beautifully woven and eloquently expressed, these stories have captivated us and made us believe that *love* is all we need to turn an ordinary life into a fairy tale come true.

What most of these stories fail to show, however, is that *love* - in all of its splendor and beauty - can also be ugly, painful, and destructive. This is especially true if you end up loving the wrong person - *which is probably why you're reading this book in the first place.*

Maybe you met someone who you thought was the answer to your prayers. Maybe he made you feel content, loved, and wanted. Maybe you were *truly* happy and stable, convinced that you had found your *person*. Maybe it was all great at the start and he seemed like everything you had ever hoped for.

But then again, maybe he would make you second-guess yourself with the way he talked down to you. Maybe you would lie awake at night, convincing yourself that his temper outbreaks were *normal*, and everyone goes through the shouting and degradation. Maybe you forced yourself to suck it up because you *loved* him, and you wanted to make sure you got your chance at happily ever after.

No doubt, being in a relationship with a narcissist can be damaging - even years after it's over. But you don't worry - I've been there.

He and I hit off like two old friends who were meeting each other again for the first time in years. We laughed like we had known each other our whole lives, so it came as no surprise that we became an official item just a few short months after our paths crossed.

Of course, it was *bliss*. Friends and family told me that they had never seen me any happier. That's because I was deep in love, and he told me he felt the same way. I couldn't help but feel confused when he started acting otherwise.

Things changed when we closed in on our first-year anniversary. Well, things had been changing for a while before then - I was just too desperate to make things work out so I forced myself to believe it was all okay.

So, when he lashed out at me and insulted my intellect, I let it slide. When he withheld emotional support when I needed it most, I told myself he just wanted to give me time. When he would belittle me, my career, and everything else that I cared about, I convinced myself he was just having a bad day.

But it kept happening. He kept hurting me, and I cried almost every day, wondering what I could have possibly done wrong. What made him change? Was *I* the problem?

It took a heartfelt conversation with my closest friends and family to finally get me to snap out of it. Apparently, I hadn't been doing a very good job of keeping my emotions contained, and they were able to see through the pain and unhappiness that the relationship caused me.

I mustered all my strength and finally told him that we were through. Naturally, he didn't take it well and had a few more ugly words to spew before we called it quits. Was it difficult? Yes, it was. Did it hurt? Yes, it did. In fact, it sometimes still does.

What I learned from being in a relationship with a narcissist is that healing and recovery takes time. These people make you fall in love, make you feel good about yourself, and earn your *trust* which is why it's easier to believe the things that they say - no matter how ugly the words might be. So once the change starts and they show their true self, your first reaction will be to cling tighter, hoping that the person you fell in love with will somehow change back and things would be how they were when it all started.

The more they change, the tighter you hold on, thinking that if you continued to show unfaltering love and loyalty, they would say sorry and change for the best. So, the vicious cycle continues, and soon enough, you'll find yourself locked in this bottomless pit of emotional torment.

Now that you're free, the destruction and pain they inflicted on you still lingers. You've probably read every resource you could find to help you learn how to deal with all the sadness and worry that your partner left behind, but none of it seems to offer the answers you were looking for.

In that case, it's a good thing you found this book.

After my romantic run in with a narcissist, I've dedicated my time and energy towards helping other women recover from the aftermath of narcissistic abuse - and this book is the pinnacle of those efforts.

So, if you're ready to heal, if you're eager to live your life without self-doubt, if you're hoping to find *love again*, then stay and read. This is how *I effectively overcame the damage of narcissistic abuse, and I'm sharing it all in this comprehensive book.*

Chapter 1 - Success Stories

The first thing that keeps a person from healing after narcissistic abuse is the thought that it's *just not possible.* It hurts too much, you miss him too much, you're just too emotionally drained to even start thinking about recovery - these are all common sentiments shared by those who are only just starting the process of healing.

While it's absolutely acceptable for you to feel defeated and uninspired, you should remember that healing can only begin *with you*. Making the choice to pick up the pieces and rebuild what was left after the destruction will start you off towards a fuller, happier life.

Of course, it might not seem impossible now. But there are *millions of women* who have survived the aftermath and managed to rise through the ashes to become their best selves. These women serve as our inspiration, making it easier for us to believe that recovery *is in fact possible.*

Gabby, 3 Years Abused, Occupational Therapist

Gabby met Stuart during her internship as part of her

Occupational Therapy program. He was a staff nurse, so they would spend quite a lot of time navigating the same floor and departments at the hospital. They say that *proximity breeds attraction*, and it seems that's exactly what happened to the couple after having been exposed to each other so often.

They went steady just as Gabby graduated from her degree, and she couldn't be happier to start this new chapter in her life with a budding career ahead of her and the love of her life by her side. But as we all know, life has a way of throwing curve balls every now and then.

Gabby struggled to get a stable job after graduation, which really wasn't what she expected. Competition was tight, and with most of the medical facilities in her area brimming with new applicants, she started to feel incompetent in the sea of fresh graduates.

On nights when she felt particularly down and defeated, she would turn to Stuart who had been her rock since they became an item. He was always supportive, always emotionally available, always ready to offer a word or two to help Gabby feel more confident in herself and her future.

But on one particular night, as she nuzzled next to him to talk about how her day had gone, he gave out a groan and complained, *"Again? We talk about this dead-end job-hunting charade literally **every night**. If you're so insecure about the competition, maybe it's because they actually **are** more capable than you."*

She was stunned. She held back her tears and asked him to repeat what he said - a request that was met with an exasperated sigh and a shrug that pulled his arm away from her hands. Gabby was so confused - *what happened?* He was usually so receptive of what she had to say.

Thinking that perhaps Stuart had a pretty rough day of his own, Gabby dusted her shoulders off and thought that maybe he just needed a little space. So that's precisely what she gave him. Unfortunately, no amount of space would fix the downward spiral they were headed in.

For the next several months, Gabby would struggle to find a job, which made her feel more and more insecure about her own capabilities. Although Stuart was usually receptive of her emotions, there were times when he would completely turn the blame on her.

Gabby started to feel upset with Stuart for shutting out her feelings and invalidating her when she sought out his comfort. So, she sat him down and talked to him in an attempt to reconcile whatever problems he might have been keeping to himself. What he said during their talk, however, wasn't what Gabby expected to hear.

Stuart blamed her "obsession" with job-hunting for the changes in their relationship. He said that she had run out of time for him, which made him feel empty and abandoned. He claimed that he felt like a second priority to a problem that shouldn't have been as big an issue as it was.

He yelled, he pointed his finger, and he insulted Gabby by telling her that her failure at finding a job was predictable based on her failure to sustain a healthy relationship. Then he walked out and slammed the door, without giving her a minute to say anything more.

Gabby started second guessing herself. *Was* she at fault for all the problems happening in her career and her relationship? Was she putting in too much time and effort into finding a job, that Stuart ended up feeling left out and abandoned? Was she being selfish?

She came up to him that evening and offered her apology, which he graciously accepted, telling her that if she wanted to sustain their partnership, she would have to try harder and put it a little more effort. So that's what Gabby did. She minimized the time she spent job-hunting and offered more of her days to being there for Stuart - whatever that meant.

Unfortunately, hanging around the hospital where Stuart worked did little for Gabby's self-esteem. She would find herself staring at professionals her age, secure and happy in the work they performed, wondering whether she would ever get the chance to serve her purpose the same way.

In a lot of ways, she admired Stuart for his capabilities when it came to his job. He was dedicated, consistent, and commendable, often receiving the praise and good words of his superiors and patients. At the peak of their arguments, Stuart would use Gabby's admiration for his work ethic as a weapon, telling her that she was only jealous of his accomplishments since she didn't have any of her own.

It went on like this for 2 years, and Gabby did nothing but accept her partner's hurtful words, not wanting to upset or insult him for things that she was convinced were her fault. Even after she finally managed to land a job, their arguments became more and more explosive, focusing on issues concerning their time and money.

At the end of the 3-year stretch since becoming official, Gabby felt lacking, incompetent, unhappy, and afraid, always doubting herself and second-guessing her capabilities. She became obsessed with pleasing her partner, thinking that all the different problems they faced were all borne of her mistakes.

Unfortunately, Stuart dealt the final blow by leaving Gabby. He had apparently found a new mate and claimed that she was far more capable than Gabby who he said was *"nothing more than a loser."* For Gabby, the pain was overwhelming, and she begged him to stay. But his mind was made up.

In the months following her breakup, she felt exceptionally low. Her depression and worry made her wonder whether allowing Stuart to leave was the right thing to do. Her career was failing as she missed more work days than she attended, and she found herself withdrawing from her closest family members and friends.

But after being encouraged to enroll in a program for individuals suffering from the aftermath of narcissistic abuse, Gabby was able to rediscover herself. More importantly, she understood what Stuart had been doing all along and how his behavior made it possible for her to accept the blame for everything that went wrong in their relationship.

Now, years after the turmoil, Gabby has become the successful occupational therapist that she always wanted to be, helping individuals who suffer from anxiety and other mental disorders as her way of paying it forward.

Wendy, 2 Years Abused, Travel Blogger

Wendy and Marty became an item when they were set up by mutual friends who thought they would be a perfect match for each other. As with any other relationship, it was that way at the beginning. They shared the same passion for adventure which made their partnership exciting, to say the least.

Another thing that they had in common was their interest in social media. Before they even met, Wendy and Marty had significantly large follower bases on a popular platform where they shared their experiences on budget travel and other fun experiences. That's how they came to decide that they would try their hand at professional travel bloggers full-time.

They pooled together their resources and after just a month of being official hit the road with nothing more than their backpacks could contain. It was exhilarating, exciting, and new, so naturally, Wendy felt as though she had made all the right choices with the right person.

Soon after landing at their first destination, they ran into a few issues concerning their accommodation and transportation, which Marty was quick to pin down on Wendy. She found it odd that he would react so violently over a mistake that she felt wasn't anyone's conscious fault, but she let the incident slide, thinking maybe he was just tired.

They would continue travelling, posting their experiences on their profiles, gaining a stronger base of followers on their individual accounts which now started to catch the attention of the companies they wanted to hook in the first place. Soon enough, Wendy was receiving offers from airline companies offering all expenses paid travel to have them featured on her page. She was over the moon.

But when she approached Marty with her good news, he shot her down. *"This isn't the airline that we wanted to partner with. So, we're not taking the deal."* Wendy was surprised. Wasn't this what they set out to do in the first place? With their funds dwindling, Wendy thought that it was *imperative* that they take on a partner as soon as possible so they could keep their little dream afloat. So, she took the deal without telling her partner.

Of course, Marty soon found out what had happened, and this became the focal point of a string of arguments that would push their relationship to its limit. Marty blamed Wendy's poor management skills for their unstable finances. He said that she was jealous of his internet success, and that she was desperate to get ahead, which is why she took on the airline offer despite Marty explicitly telling her not to.

When Wendy attempted to answer back, he lashed out at her by telling her that she was self-serving and uncaring. He said that if she had only listened to all his commands from the start, then they wouldn't be in the mess they were in. After all, he asserted, between the two of them, he was more successful in terms of their social media efforts, so he claimed that he had a better understanding of how things worked.

Wendy spent the night out on the beachfront that evening, wanting to stay away from Marty whose explosive nature made itself known to her for the first time. She examined all the things he said and started to doubt herself. *He was right*, she thought. And she convinced herself that the only way to make things right was to follow what he said without fuss.

Every time a new paid partnership wiggled its way into Wendy's inbox, Marty would tell her to reject the offer. He claimed that the only ones worth accepting were those that coursed their proposals through him, so Wendy would have to redirect all of the companies that approached her to communicate with Marty instead if they wanted their offers to be accepted.

Unfortunately, the majority of these companies wanted to establish a partnership with Wendy *alone* since their brands were more interested in associating with a female influencer. So, in any case, Marty wouldn't even have to be a part of the partnership.

Marty learned this soon after and lashed out at Wendy once again. He called her arrogant, greedy, and manipulative. He said that without him, Wendy wouldn't even be where she was. He yelled at her, belittled her contributions, and finally ended the episode by slamming the door on Wendy's face. He would proceed to ignore her for several days after the event.

One evening, as Wendy was returning to their hotel room from dinner alone, she saw Marty cozying up to other women at the resort bar. She walked up to him and asked if she could speak with him for a moment, and he responded by looking at her and saying he was busy.

She was hurt. Marty was deliberately acting out to make her feel unloved and unimportant, which caused Wendy to break down in their room for hours. When he arrived, he looked at her, slumped in one corner of the room, and went about preparing for bed as though he hadn't seen in her in the first place. It crushed Wendy to see him so emotionally distant, especially after having done all she could to keep their goals in sight.

That evening, she called her friends back home and told them everything that had happened over the 2 years that they were on the road. They told her to leave. With every ounce of her will, and the weight of reluctance on her shoulders, Wendy took on the deals that were pending in her inbox and left the resort to move on to her next destination without Marty.

There, she tore herself away from the world and focused her mind and energy on herself. She took a break from social media and tried to meditate on her life and her aspirations. While it hurt her to have to leave her partner, she knew now that he was toxic, and that his behavior was holding her back from living her best life.

Wendy continued to establish a successful career as a travel blogger, learning about other cultures around the world and making friends everywhere she went. Although the opportunity to fall in love again did come up quite a few times since her breakup, Wendy promised herself that she would give herself time to heal completely before she engaged in new relationship. She learned the value of investing in herself before anything else, which sparked a brand-new sense of self-worth and confidence that she could never find anywhere else.

Laura, 5 Years Abused, Business Owner

It's harder to get out of a narcissistic relationship if you're anchored down by marriage and children, which is precisely the situation that Laura was in. She couldn't remember when Michael started showing signs of narcissism, but she could recall that their relationship had already been on the rocks since before they said their vows.

Their story was the typical high-school sweetheart love story - they met in high-school and stayed a couple all the way through college. Laura was deeply invested in Michael and reveled in the idea that he would be her first and last.

All throughout their relationship, arguments would come and go. Usually, Michael would withdraw completely from her, giving her the cold shoulder for weeks until she finally came up to him with an apology. Most of their arguments revolved around the same thing - *time*.

Laura often felt like a second or even third priority to Michael. He would go out of his way to see friends, make plans with coworkers, and visit close female friends. All the while, Laura had to *beg* him to give her the same importance, which would often result in Michael pointing out how needy and demanding she was.

"I don't always see these people, and this is how I want to spend my time. I'm tired of you trying to control my every move," he would say. But Laura knew that it had been a while since the last time they went on a date, since they last shared a quiet dinner together, or since they did anything new. Whenever she would bring it up though, he would call

her clingy and needy, and then turn her away once more with his cold shoulder.

Laura lived with Michael's behavior for years, and despite the rocky relationship, they tied the knot after 3 years of being a couple. Needless to say, things didn't change even after having tied the knot.

Michael and Laura entered the winter seasons of their marriage shortly after the sound of blissful wedding bells faded away. Michael was always away with friends, and Laura was powerless to ask him for time and attention in fear that he might lash out and argue. So, she spent most of her time at home, since they had both agreed that she would remain a housewife.

While Laura refused to talk about her marital issues with anyone, it was clear to her that Michael preferred being in control of everything. This is why she believed he muscled her into staying at home instead of working, despite the fact that they were yet to have any children.

Laura would spend most of her time focusing on hobbies and caring after their home. At night, Michael would arrive, have dinner with her, talk about his day, and ask her sweetly to come to bed with him, which would always reassure Laura of his affections.

Soon enough, they would welcome their first baby, and with tears in their eyes, Michael told Laura that seeing their son for the first time was the happiest moment in his life. He told her that he was proud of what she had done and that he would do whatever he could to make sure they both had a seamless transition into parenthood. While Laura hoped it would be the beginning of positive change, it soon became apparent that the birth of their son would cause some of the worst arguments they had ever had.

Laura was exhausted from tending to their newborn, and she felt that Michael was hardly spending any time with the baby. So, one evening she asked if he could take the night shift, since it would be the weekend the next day. From his office chair he looked at her and asked her if she had any idea what she was requesting from him.

He said that he was working hard 5 days a week to make sure all their needs were met, and that he rarely ever got the recognition he deserved for being such a dependable provider. He claimed that Laura was a nagger who had nothing good to say about him and who demanded too much of his time and energy. He closed off his argument by telling her that he was probably more exhausted than she was, and that she was simply far less capable of performing under pressure which is why she felt the need to come to him for help.

Laura expected that kind of reaction from him but hoped anyway that he would understand her this one instance. Unfortunately, Michael's true nature would once again get the best of him, and now they found themselves in the same situation.

They had a second baby just as their eldest turned 1 year old, and that's when things started to really get problematic. Laura had developed anxiety issues, thinking that she was the reason for the difficulties they experienced in their marriage. She became desperate for Michael's attention and compassion, which pushed her into a downward spiral of submissiveness.

She was obsessed with pleasing Michael, even if it meant depriving herself of rest and other basic needs. She would offer him a massage as he got home every night, slave over the stove to prepare his favorite meals, and simply fulfill everything that she thought was necessary to maintain herself a "good wife" in his eyes.

Of course, there were times that Laura would slip up. She would unknowingly do things that upset Michael, and she would be blamed for how he felt - regardless of how small the issue might have been. This would cause Laura to beat herself up over the little altercation for days.

One evening, as her husband was away on a business trip, Laura called up her mother and asked if she could come over to watch the kids while she took a few hours to sleep. Of course, her mother obliged and was at her door shortly after they put the phone down.

She noticed Laura's defeated demeanor and asked her if there was anything she wanted to talk about. For a while, Laura kept mum and tried to redirect the conversation because she knew her mother wouldn't believe her. After all,

Michael had done a very good job at keeping his image clean with his in-laws. But as her mother egged her on for an explanation, Laura broke down crying.

She opened up about how her husband made her feel like garbage whenever she did something that slightly upset him. She talked about her self-doubt, and her self-esteem which she felt was now completely destroyed. While her mother was in shock, she knew that the only advice she could give was to tell Laura to cut the relationship off.

For Laura, the decision wasn't as easy. With 2 children, she found it difficult to make any decisions that could potentially harm their future. She didn't want them to grow up without a father. But she knew that her mental health could only take so much trauma.

So instead, she worked with her mother to find a therapy center that would cater to her depleted self-esteem and anxiety issues. She told Michael that she was enrolling herself to help her cope with post-partum depression, because she knew he wouldn't take well to the idea of her getting help for being in a narcissistic relationship.

Over the course of a few months, Laura was able to develop the right coping mechanisms to help her become more secure in her self-worth. She learned where he was coming from and why he acted the way he did. The classes also helped her realize that she was *never the problem*, and that her husband's reactions had nothing to do with her.

After 5 years of living through her husband's abusive behavior, Laura finally got the clarity she needed in order to take Michael's abuse in stride. Of course, she would still feel hurt at times. But ultimately, she learned more about herself and her inherent value that no man - even her husband - could take away. So, after another year, Laura had finally decided that enough was enough. She confidently took her children and served divorce papers to save herself from the stress, anxiety, and abuse.

Was it an easy divorce? No. Michael put up a very aggressive fight and tried to make it as hard as possible for Laura to get what she wanted. But at the end of the day, Laura was able to free herself from the prison her ex-husband had built with the realization that she would be much happier raising her children in a healthy single-parent home than a destructive one where her husband lived.

Today, Laura has discovered her strengths and put her talents toward managing her own thriving business which she uses to pay for her children's education, her mortgage, and her little weekend luxuries that she makes sure to indulge in.

You Can Recover

If there's one thing to take away from these 3 stories, it's that everyone can have the chance at a better life if they give themselves the opportunity. While narcissistic abuse can have you feeling like a complete failure, you need to understand that whatever feelings might have surfaced as a result of the abuse may not be true.

Narcissists have a way of tearing down their partner and making them believe false concepts about themselves. So, whether you choose to stay or hit the road, it's imperative that you reconstruct your self-concept in order to truly understand how the abuse might have falsely affected how you see yourself.

Chapter 2 - Victim Mode

Fresh from an ended relationship with a narcissist, it's possible that you might feel confused. *Did I do the right thing? Did I overreact?* It's only normal to question yourself and your motives especially if you were in a relationship with someone who did well to cover their tracks and make everything seem like it was all your fault.

What Makes it Hard to Heal?

What most individuals who have recovered from narcissistic

relationships claim is that the first few steps through healing are the most difficult. With a multitude of questions running through your mind, it can be a challenge to make sense of your relationship and why it didn't work out.

There are a few factors that can make it even more difficult to move on from the damage but maintaining awareness of them can make it easier to move beyond the initial confusion.

A Disparity of Truth

The first challenge that can get in the way of your recovery is the apparent disparity between *what you believed* and *what was true*. If you were in a relationship with a narcissist who was particularly capable of covering his tracks, then he may have deflected a lot (if not all) of the blame to make you feel like you were at fault for everything that happened.

Clarity in Retrospect

Looking back at your relationship, you'll now start to see all the different red flags as though you're only experiencing everything for the first time. What's difficult about this part of the process is that it makes you question your intellect - *anyone else would have seen those problems, so why didn't I?*

Now that you know your partner was a narcissist, you'll start to see all their reactions and behaviors, and how truly destructive they were in nature. The hard part is realizing how many times you *let* your partner hurt and damage you because you trusted them and loved them despite the toxicity of their actions.

What makes this part particularly painful is that it forces you to relive all the painful moments of the past. Revisiting memories and seeing them in their true light can be exceptionally hurtful, especially if you were originally convinced that your significant other loved and cared for you.

The Pit of Self Criticism

One of the reasons why narcissists have such long-lasting effects on their victims is because they feast on your self-concept. They make you think all of these negative things about yourself and force you to accept the blame for everything that goes wrong in your relationship and your personal life.

Even after ending a relationship with a narcissist, these feelings of incompetence and self-loathing can continue, which is why you might end up blaming yourself for not *seeing* the red flags earlier on. *How could I have been so stupid? It was my fault for not seeing the signs sooner.*

It's normal to want to find someone to blame in an effort to reconcile the past. But keep in mind that *you* were never the problem. Narcissists are gifted at twisting the truth and feeding you lies about yourself, so don't think for one second that you're lacking, incapable, idiotic, or at fault.

Learned Powerlessness

Narcissists need to feel in command, so they look for someone they can push around and trample on to inflate their own feelings of self-esteem. As their "scape goat", you might have fed them that need. This would entail bowing out of arguments, accepting the blame, and blocking out the situation by muting out whatever is happening around you. This puts you in a trans-like state, allowing you to get around with your usual tasks without having to confront the reality of your situation.

Now that you're out of the toxic relationship, you might still be in the same condition. This powerlessness to *act* out of your own free will in an attempt to mute out the world around you and the pain of your narcissistic abuse can make it feel impossible to regain control of your situation.

A Lonely Road

Victims of narcissistic abuse will often run to their family and friends for support during tough times. But because narcissists are exceptionally good at maintaining a trustworthy, clean image of themselves for the people around him, friends and family will often find it hard to believe that you're being hurt or victimized no matter how hard you try to explain your situation.

So maybe when you sought comfort from your parents, siblings, or your closest friends, you might not have gotten the response you were looking for. You may have even been met with comments that completely invalidate your experiences, telling you that you're probably just having a bad day.

Don't worry - your situation is *real*, your pain is *valid*, and your problems were never your own fault. It might be difficult to tread the road on your own, but there are lots of support groups and communities that can offer you the comfort you need to successfully complete the healing process.

Fear of the Unknown

What happens now? What about the future? Will you ever find love again? For married people, when will the divorce process end? And how will the children cope? It's true, moving on from a narcissistic relationship might be *harder* than coping with any regular breakup because of the damage that you might have sustained to your self-worth.

A narcissist convinces you that you're worthless and incapable - that you're at fault for the issues of your relationship. So, your tendency might have been to cling on to him in fear that *everything might fall apart* if you did anything against his will.

Now that he's out of your life, you're left to make a lot of the decisions on your own. After long-term narcissistic abuse, that might be one of the most challenging things you'll ever have to do. How do you proceed? And what will happen when you start calling the shots?

Remember that before you and your ex got together, *you were your own functional human being.* You had a life before all of this, and you can resume your existence without having to depend on someone who finds satisfaction in controlling your every move.

Laying Down the Facts

On the road to recovery, there are a few facts that you need to lay out for yourself in order to help yourself get a better grasp of reality as it is. These facts give a better understanding not only of your ex and your past relationship, but also to help you plant your feet firmly on the ground so you have the footing you need in order to sprint through the healing process.

Don't Expect Them to Change

It might have crossed your mind more than once to rekindle your relationship with a narcissist, because you felt that would end your misery. Unfortunately, this never seems to be the answer since most research shows that *narcissists are near incapable of change.*

On a general note, everyone should be able to change their ways - given that they're genuinely interested in improving. Of course, the initiative to change starts with the realization that there's something wrong with how they've behaved in the past. With the narcissistic prototype, that's almost impossible since a deformed self-concept is one of their major flaws.

It would take years and years of individual therapy to be able to rewire a narcissist especially if the roots of their issues stem as far back as their childhood. Unless you're truly invested in this person, such as most women who *married* a narcissist, you might be better off thinking of your own well-being by leaving the toxic relationship and finding someone who can meeting your emotional needs.

You Were Never the Problem

Perhaps one of the hardest things about breaking up with a narcissist that you truly loved is seeing him establish a new relationship with another woman. At a glance, he might seem happier than he ever was with you, which can reinforce the feelings of incompetence. But before you believe the hype, take the time to remember that he probably did the same thing with you.

His new displays of affection and love are not a way to hurt you further - he's probably forgotten all about you by now. This is simply the indication that he's starting a brand-new cycle with his new victim. Narcissists *need* to establish that initial atmosphere of a loving, caring relationship because that's how they develop the leverage over their partners in the first place.

Soon enough, they'll be treating their new victim the same way they were treating you. But just like your relationship, it's unlikely that outsiders - including yourself - will see the true nature of the partnership from a third-person point of view.

So yes, at a glance, they'll look happy and satisfied, like nothing could ever go wrong with their relationship. And yes, this might make you think that your ex's bad behavior was solely reserved for you, but don't let those negative thoughts take a hold on you. *You* were never the problem, and the poor treatment wasn't uniquely for you. Your ex hasn't changed. It's just the start of a new cycle.

You Shouldn't Feel Sorry for Him

One of the reasons why it's such a challenge for victims to let go of their narcissistic ex is because they feel their partner's behavior was a cry for help. Narcissistic behaviors are often thought of as an expression of a lack of self-esteem, which espouses the need to bring other people down to make their low sense of self-worth more manageable. While that might be true for *some* narcissists, it's really more common to encounter grandiose, malignant narcissists.

At the complete opposite end of the spectrum, grandiose narcissists *truly believe* they're superior to everyone else, and that this sense of inflated self-worth gives them the right to trample on others. The purpose of their cruel acts is simply for their personal pleasure. They *enjoy* manipulating others and find satisfaction in the destruction they cause.

For the most part, what fuels a narcissist's actions is the feeling that they're entitled to it because they're *better* than everyone else. So, if they see that you are financially secure, career driven, outwardly beautiful, or anything else that might be a threat to their self-concept of being the *best*, they'd gladly tear you down for it to maintain their spot at the top.

They Know What They're Doing

Maybe he didn't mean to hurt me. Another way that victims try to clear a narcissist of blame is by assuming that they were unaware of the pain that they were inflicting. This makes it easier to *forgive* the offender, by propping them up to be innocent and unaware of the cruel things they do.

Before you let that idea dictate the rest of your actions, remember that individuals in narcissistic relationships are told to *avoid any sort of couple's therapy or counselling.* Why? When put in a position that might shed light on their true nature, narcissists can present themselves as the *victim*.

So, in the face of a counselor or therapist, your partner will likely draw attention to your flaws and errors, making you the focal point and the reason behind a lot of the troubles in your relationship. If the therapist you're consulting isn't well versed with narcissistic abuse, they may fall for the charade.

This can be detrimental to the victim, causing significant distress and confusion. I mean, with a counselor hot on your heels and telling *you* to change your ways, you might start to question whether you were fault-free all along.

What does any of this have to do with a narcissist's knowledge of what he's doing? It's simple - anyone inflicting abuse or pain on another person shouldn't be able to just *turn it off* when there's someone who might see the reality *if* they weren't aware of what they were doing.

That said, since a narcissistic partner can change their demeanor and make themselves look like the victim in the face of a therapist, it only means they're aware of what they're doing in the first place.

For you, this means *accepting the reality*. They **did mean to hurt you**, and it did satisfy him to control and inflict pain on you. So, celebrate your freedom from the relationship and try to invest in your new-found self-worth instead.

The Cornerstones of Healing

Everyone is different, so there are a variety of recovery techniques developed to help each individual victim achieve healing as efficiently as possible. Despite the differences, however, there are a few *healing cornerstones* that work for everyone across the board.

These methods aren't *exact* remedies in and of themselves, but they are ideal ancillary techniques that can help improve the results you get out of your other efforts.

Ask Why

I felt betrayed, toyed with, and used. I was made to look like a fool by the one person that I truly loved and trusted.

While it's absolutely valid for you to be feeling these emotions, at this early phase in healing, it's more important that you ask why instead of what. Understanding why you felt a certain way instead of trying to pick out what you were feeling at specific points in your relationship can make it easier for you to label your feelings.

In effect, this makes it easier for you to be in control of your emotions throughout the process. Seeing the why's behind the strong feelings that you went through also helps bring light to the cruel acts that your ex might have put you through. This objective point of view should allow you to deal with recovery more efficiently, eliminating the chances of reliving the pain with each processed memory.

Be Specific

The negative feelings you have towards your ex can make it particularly easy to brand all people the same way. The idea that *all men (or women)* will treat you the same way can breed a feeling of resentment and hate, sparking a bitterness that will make it difficult for you to release negative feelings and possibly engage in a new relationship in the future.

Instead of generalizing the concepts you discover and applying them to all the potential mates around you, consider the fact that your ex *is still a unique individual*. His mistakes aren't *everyone else's,* so be careful not to brand others the same way.

Be Kind to Yourself

It's easy to shame yourself and feel embarrassed or upset about how things turned out between you and your ex. Before you let any of those feelings stir up new negative ideas, remember to *love* yourself.

You should be the first person to be compassionate towards yourself in this situation - especially because you might not receive the same sentiments from family and friends who are conditioned to believe that your partner was a good guy who treated you fairly.

Keep in mind that you *aren't* stupid or idiotic for allowing this person into your life - you were never the first nor the last to experience this kind of hurt and pain. You *aren't* uniquely incapable of detecting a narcissist, they're just simply that hard to decode.

Finally, *you aren't your experiences*. Don't let the negative emotions define who you are. Always remember to keep yourself at a distance when dealing with the painful experiences you went through with your partner.

Maintain objectivity - look at things the way they were and try to avoid latching on to bitterness. This will make it easier for you to process everything without having to relive the pain every time.

Be Smart

Lots of narcissistic relationships end on a bad note, especially because abusive partners will never take the blame for any of the issues that may have arisen throughout. If you still need to maintain communication with your narcissistic partner, such as during a divorce or custody battle, do not re-engage in arguments.

Shouting, bad mouthing, insulting, and other derogatory acts fired *towards* you are used as bait to keep you coming back. This is what your narcissistic ex wants because it gives him the leverage to control your reactions once again.

Don't feed into his plans, and instead record anything and everything he might say - especially when spewed argumentatively or threateningly. These could help you win your custody battle.

Essentially, you shouldn't give him any more rope to cling to. If you *stop* feeding him the line, he'll lose his grip on you and ultimately realize that there's nothing left of your relationship that he can use to his advantage.

Stay on Top

It's true that falling off your wagon as you go through the process of recovery can be very possible. You still love him, you still want to make things work, or you still feel hurt and shame from all the mean and cruel things he did to you. It's normal, and no one is asking you to feel otherwise.

But you need to understand that these feelings can destroy your recovery and prevent you from moving on into a happier life with the fullness and joy that you've been looking for. So, you need to stay on top of your feelings and keep them under control if you feel that they're starting to get out of hand.

One of the most ideal ways that you can do this is by *starting a journal*. Writing down your feelings as they come helps you acknowledge the reality of your situation without basking in the negative emotions that it might produce. As you write, you release pent up negativities and give yourself a shame and guilt-free space where you can talk about your feelings without judgement.

As you move through the process of recovery, you can even revisit your journals to see just how far you've come in terms of emotional healing and growth.

Journal Writing Exercises

When we write, we often let go of our inhibitions and share deep-seated emotions that might not have surfaced through mere conversation. Thus, jotting them down can bring hidden feelings to light, allowing you to truly understand your own situation and how to deal with the damage that you've been dealt.

To start off your journal writing practice, consider answering one or two of these questions daily.

What are some of the qualities that you expect or prefer to see in an ideal partner? In what ways did your ex meet these expectations, and in what ways did they fail?

How do you feel about your current situation? Are you still fearful that your ex might be able to control you in some ways? What do you think it would take for you to feel completely safe?

Who are the people in your support group? How do they fulfill your needs in terms of comfort and reassurance? Do you feel that there's anything else you need to help improve the support you're receiving?

Where do you see yourself 5 years from now in terms of your emotional recovery? What do you think you need to do in order to fulfill that goal?

Chapter 3 - Getting Rid of the Pseudo Personality

During the first few months after I ended my relationship with my narcissistic partner, I felt the need to talk about my experiences to everyone I could manage to speak with. I would recount the abuse over and over and express my anger repeatedly because I felt that's what I needed in order to feel better.

Months passed, and I noticed that whenever I revisited the experience, I would feel the same anger and shame. Nothing had *truly* changed. So, I started to examine my methods - why wasn't I experiencing the relief and healing that I thought I would by this point in time?

After some research, I learned that what I had been doing wasn't actually ideal. I thought that just by talking about my experiences, I would release negative emotions and move on effectively. But what was actually happening was just shallow story telling - people *learned about* my story, but there was no actual healing happening.

Developing a *deeper* understanding of what you feel is paramount to recovery because it lets you dissect your emotions. *Why* you feel a specific way is more important than knowing *what* you felt, helping you uncover the reasons behind emotions so you can properly resolve them and cut them at the root.

Acknowledging Your Pseudo Personality

Your abuser likely made you feel loved, important, and secure during the start of your relationship, but began to insult your capabilities, your worth, and your confidence a few months into your partnership. During these arguments, you probably heard some pretty nasty things being said about you in general.

Personally, my narcissistic partner would insult my intellect and tell me frequently that if I hadn't been so *stupid*, we would be much happier and problem-free. It made me feel completely idiotic, and I *believed* he was right for the longest time.

This is because he had *earned* my trust. By showing me all the things I wanted to see in my partner before he started tearing me down, I felt like he was speaking from an informed point of view. Like he genuinely knew me better than others around us, so his opinions about me - even the ugly ones - were easy to believe.

In a narcissistic relationship, these nasty comments can

develop what's called a *pseudo personality*. That is, you begin to believe the lies about yourself and develop a new self-concept that doesn't really reflect who you are. Some of the most common personality traits that victims assume may include:

- Clumsy
- Stupid
- Uncertain
- Anxious
- Disobedient
- Lacking common sense
- Uncaring
- Inconsiderate

Keep in mind that *all these traits* including many others that you may have been abused with, do **not accurately define you**. While you might have started to believe that these are qualities you possess, it's important to remind yourself that your abuser **wanted you to think poorly of yourself** which is why he may have pushed you to believe false concepts about who you are.

Tearing down your identity and making you believe that you're a bad or incapable person helps a narcissist maintain his death grip on you. By using these words against you constantly, you're likely to feel that you *owe* them for your "bad behavior." The uglier your self-concept becomes, the more likely you'll try to stick around and pay them back for all the remiss and problems they claim you caused.

Although it can be difficult to remember life before the abuse, there are ways that you can rediscover your *true* self. It starts off by acknowledging the changes that have occurred as the result of your narcissist ex's behavior.

The Challenge of Dealing with a Pseudo Personality

The main reason for the difficulty caused by the pseudo personality is the fact that it makes you *dependent* on your abuser - just as they intended. It requires that you verify all your feelings, actions, and thoughts by checking *first* if they coincide with the very strict parameters of *correctness* that the abuser has set.

Take for example the case of *Wendy* from the first chapter. After Marty had made it clear that he didn't want her taking any new partnerships or deals without his consent, Wendy was forced into submissiveness. She would run each new offer by Marty before she made any moves on her own - even if she knew that accepting the deals would have been more attuned to their original intentions.

Victims often feel the need to *appease* the needs and desires of their abusers. In many ways, it can be two-fold. The first reason is to keep their narcissistic partner *happy* because it keeps the ugly, abusive, and critical facet of their personality at bay. By following their rules, a victim can maintain the light and problem-free air of their relationship.

The second reason why victims try so hard to walk the line is because it keeps their image *clean*. As you might already know, dealing with a narcissist means you shift between two different character generalizations. So, to the abuser, you're either **all good** or **all bad**. Being *all bad* means being at the receiving end of a barrage of criticism, derogatory treatment, and rejection. Being *all good* means you get to enjoy the sunny, happy days of the relationship where the narcissist would treat you in a way that makes you feel deserving of love and comfort.

The pseudo personality that you've developed through the course of the relationship helps fulfill your abuser's requirements. Think of it as an internal verifier that prevents you from getting on the narcissist's bad side.

Should you do that? How would they react? Should you think that? Does it coincide with your partner's thoughts? Should you feel that way? Does it put your abuser in a bad light?

This subconscious mechanism was put into motion over the

course of your relationship and was slowly cemented in place with each new opportunity that the narcissist took to degrade and insult you. Now, it serves the purpose of keeping you in line even *without conscious effort* to control you from the abuser's end.

The challenge now is dismantling the pseudo personality to help your *true self* break through. But how do you destroy a mechanism that runs on self-doubt? How do you reprogram yourself if the program you're currently on works to keep you from making self-driven decisions?

Breaking the Machination

Freeing yourself from the mechanism created by your abuser will make it possible for you to decide *for your own best interest* instead of *for the approval and acceptance of your abuser or others around you.* There are a few steps you can take in order to rediscover yourself.

Stop Contradicting Yourself

As you heal, you'll probably come to conclude that your entire situation was the result of your partner's narcissistic tendencies. I'm not even going to stop you from thinking that because it's likely the truth. *At this point, there is no benefit or need in trying to absolve your abuser of their cruel actions. Give them the full blame because that's how it should be!*

The contradiction lies in the fact that you might start to tell yourself a few generalizations that go against that initial thought. For instance, you might say things like, *"I should have walked away sooner,"* or *"I was too stupid to see what was happening."*

Contradicting yourself creates confusion and prevents you from completely tearing down the mechanism that has been set into action in your subconscious. What's more, you were likely *pure and honest* in terms of your intentions for your relationship so there's no need to turn the blame on yourself.

Was there ever a time that you deliberately did anything with malicious intent? With the objective to inflict pain and shame? If the answer is no, then that means you were *genuinely* acting out of love and concern. So, it doesn't matter how things turned out or how you were made to think about yourself - *you were being real to yourself and your partner, and you only had your relationship's best interest in mind.*

The first step in destroying the machination is absolving no one other than **yourself** from the blame. You've been made the enemy long enough - it's time you recognize that *you were never at fault!* As soon as you come to realize and accept that, you'll find it easier to discover your real self.

Reflect on Your Behavior

Although it might be painful and difficult to revisit the past, you may benefit from reflecting on the way you were made to act throughout the duration of your relationship. *Do you notice any consistencies in your reactions to your ex?*

For instance, when I reflected on my own actions, I noticed I would usually be particularly cautious of my choices if they concerned finances. This is because my abuser was exceptionally talented when it came to money matters, so he really felt like it was something he had the upper hand in.

When we finally called it quits, I found myself having a significantly difficult time making monetary decisions on my own. I would constantly second-guess my choices and think that I was squandering financial resources on unnecessary luxuries - even if they were absolutely needed!

The point in *seeing* the facets of life where the mechanism is particularly well-established will make it easier for you to understand how it *controls* your decisions. For me, the subconscious flow chart was strongest in terms of my finances and household maintenance because these were the main focus of most of our arguments.

Now that you can clearly depict the specific areas of life that the mechanism is most apparent, examine how it makes you act. For me, it was a lot of doubt and indecisiveness. I could never come to a decision without having to go back and forth to question my choices. There was a time I would even consult Google for something *as personal* as *how to spend my finances!*

Then you can dissect your behavior to give more objectivity to your situation. For instance, *why am I so afraid to spend my money without taking cues from others around me? Were there any instances when I actually put myself in danger or in harm's way by the daily monetary decisions I made?*

Once you start to see that your own, self-driven decisions aren't actually as ill-advised or destructive as you've been led to believe, you'll start to break down the doubt that was set into motion. Although it might take a while, constantly taking the time to review your motives and see how they might have been put in question in the first place can help remove the subconscious shackles.

Begin Self-Discovery

Possibly the most important and helpful thing you can do to release yourself from your pseudo personality is to begin your journey to self-discovery. I know, it sounds obscure. But there are some very doable and realistic steps you can take to help rediscover who you really are.

One way that really helped me was by starting a *self-discovery journal.* Writing exercises that allow you to uncover how you would act or decide without your subconscious taking control of your every move.

Here are a few writing exercises you can try to help you become more aware of your true self.

What makes you feel most anxious or fearful? Can you give at least 3 objective reasons why these fears are rational or realistic?

If you could be anywhere at this very moment, where would you like to be and why? Can you describe how you might spend your day at this ideal location?

When do you feel happiest? Name some activities or experiences that make you feel genuinely joyful and content.

If you had a million bucks fall into your lap right now, what would you spend it on? Try not to think about it too much and be spontaneous!

Find a picture of yourself from before your abusive relationship and describe the version of yourself in that image. Next, find a picture of yourself during the narcissistic relationship and compare your two selves. What changed?

Chapter 4 - Inner Child Healing

From Freud to Erikson, the number of psychologists and psychoanalysts supporting the importance of our childhood shaping our adult psyche are countless. You might already know that your narcissistic ex actually became that way through specific childhood experiences and had a potentially poor relationship with his parents.

But this guide on inner child healing is much less about your abuser's past and more about *your own.* Why? Certain aspects of your earlier years could have molded you to become particularly prone to emotional abuse. Picking out these parts of your childhood can make it possible for you to avoid possibly re-engaging with another narcissist in the future.

How Does it Happen?

Those most prone to emotional abuse as adults are people who were abused as children. Now, your concept of your parents may be pristine and I'm not trying to tell you they were anything less than the best parents they could be. However, there are a variety of kinds of child abuse and they can be inflicted at varying degrees.

When I first tried to examine my childhood, I found myself feeling very defensive. My parents were nothing less than the most hard-working people I had ever known, so it was difficult for me to see them in any other way. Plus, I didn't want to *blame* them for the situation I found myself in with my narcissistic ex.

But as I opened up to the idea of childhood issues and how they don't necessarily depict *bad parents*, I started to notice some possible reasons for the vulnerability. Firstly, my parents were both hospital workers. My mother was a nurse and my father was a surgeon's assistant. They spent most of their time at the hospital and came home tired in the wee hours of morning.

As an adult, I know it was only because they were working hard to give me the best possible future. But as I dug deeper, I did start to notice that my *childhood* self didn't see it the same way.

I realized that I often found myself wishing they had more time for me, especially because I didn't have any brothers or sisters. I was hungry for their companionship and attention, but I knew it wasn't something I could just ask for because of their busy schedules.

On top of that, I came to realize that their demanding jobs also made them withdrawn or slightly hostile to me at times. Of course, I was a kid and I had a lot of questions lined up for them whenever I got the chance to talk to them. Unfortunately, their tired bodies couldn't always accommodate my persistent and often annoying inquiries, so they would either dismiss me and ask not to be disturbed or they wouldn't hear me all together.

This often made me feel neglected, but I didn't hold it against them. I simply learned to live in my home's silence and the loneliness that came as the result of my parents' busy lives. When I became an adult, that lack of parent attachment manifested itself as neediness which became the ideal quality for someone seeking to *control* their partner.

There are lots of different types of "abuse", and some - like my experiences - might not be as overt as others. While you might want to believe that your parents had nothing to do with your narcissistic relationship, it's important to recognize how their parenting style might have contributed to your vulnerability.

Does it make them bad people? Of course not. Unless they were deliberately abusing you, minor remiss on your parents' end doesn't and shouldn't brand them negatively. It should simply serve as your guide towards developing a deeper understanding of who you are and why you're prone to abuse.

The Inner Child in Adulthood

While I don't want to get too technical, it's important to

make mention of the *epigenetic principle*. Essentially, this psychological concept claims that the human psyche develops based from a *step-by-step process*. What that means is that the progress of the next step depends on what was achieved in previous, lower levels. Failure to properly execute the goals of the stage prior could result to issues in the execution of the next.

Basically, this means that if there were any problems in your childhood, it's highly likely that they might manifest in different ways throughout your adulthood. For instance, someone who develops a dependence on *oral stimulation* like smoking, drinking, or taking oral narcotics might have had issues going back as far as their oral exploratory phase.

Maybe they weren't breastfed enough, maybe they were frequently scolded for biting their mother while nursing, maybe they didn't receive enough oral exploration opportunities. While these might seem trivial at the childhood level, they can produce lifelong effects.

Certain childhood experiences that seep into your adulthood can make you prone to abusive relationships. Physical and emotional neglect, sexual, physical, and verbal abuse, and other adverse childhood experiences can mold your adult self and force you into specific behavioral patterns.

As you grow older, childhood experiences shift and develop into its adult counterpart. In my case, the emotional neglect became a hunger for attention and time, which my narcissistic ex found easy to exploit. All he had to do was *give me what I craved for* when he thought I deserved it and then *withhold it from me when he felt that I wasn't meeting his standards or requirements.*

Those who experience more profound abuse would be far more dependent on their partners. Unfortunately, unless your chosen mate is kind, caring, and compassionate, this *dependent* personality combined with a narcissistic partner can be a recipe for disaster.

Take for example *Reese* who was the product of a broken home. Her father was incarcerated when she was just 5 years old, and her mother divorced him shortly after. She would then grow up to watch her mother jump from partner to partner, sometimes leaving home for weeks at a time, leaving Reese alone to care for her 2 younger sisters.

When they became teens, Reese's mother continued her reckless, absentee behavior. Unfortunately for Reese, one of her sisters grew up to adopt the same difficult personality, and Reese would often find herself walking the cold streets at night in search of her carefree sister.

Throughout her growing years, Reese felt like it was her responsibility to *keep everything together*. In adulthood, this manifested as a fear of abandonment. So, when Reese fell into a relationship with a narcissist, she felt threatened and scared every time they would argue because she thought it might *push him away and cause him to leave.*

Reese equated her happiness and sense of security with a

partner who wouldn't leave her the same way she felt her family had abandoned her as a child and teen. She forced herself into submissiveness and obedience in order to prevent any threat of being left.

Unfortunately for her, her narcissistic partner *knew exactly how to exploit her fears.* So, whenever she was even slightly "out of line", all he had to do was pull out the old "I'm leaving card," and she would beg him to stay.

What Does a Stable Childhood Look Like?

There is no such thing as the perfect childhood, because there's no such thing as the perfect parent. But those who come pretty close to perfect have very few hang-ups as adults, and may very well be able to avoid narcissistic abuse because they're not as easy to exploit.

A person who feels secure in childhood will have a stronger sense of self-worth and confidence - one that's not as easily destroyed by just anyone. So, this means that the individual won't likely agree to being talked down to or degraded because they have a firm grasp of their own self-esteem.

Does this mean they're not likely to fall in love with a narcissist? Quite the contrary - anyone can fall into that trap.

Remember, narcissists are the great pretenders, able to make themselves appear a certain way in order to earn the trust, respect, and love of their victims. They're master manipulators, so even the most well-rounded people aren't exempt from their wicked wiles.

The benefit of having a secure, healthy childhood however, is that you become less likely to allow the abuse. For instance, *Kira* grew up as the youngest in a brood of 4. Her father was a humble barber shop owner and her mother was a stay-at-home mom who would sell her fresh fruit at the local farmer's market on Saturdays.

They were a lower-middle class family, but she and all her siblings managed to finish college. While she did witness her parents argue quite a few times when she was growing up, she was a firm believer of the fidelity and resilience of their marriage.

Kira grew up to be a successful bank manager, and she got that way thanks to her hard-work and diligent work ethic. She was secure in her success and knew that she was a stable, self-sustaining, responsible adult.

So, when her boyfriend of 5 months started talking down to her for allegedly *spending too much time at work*, she wasn't keen on accepting his insults. He frequently called her a boring workaholic who had no idea how to have fun, and he often gave her the cold shoulder if she refused to take work days off to spend time away with him.

Kira stood her ground because she believed she was doing the right thing for herself and her future. Over the course of the next several weeks, she felt her affection for David growing tired and cold. And soon enough, without the need for prompts, she had made the decision to call their relationship off. David was furious, claiming that Kira was a prude and that if anyone had the right to break it off, it was him.

Unfortunately for this narcissist, Kira was just too certain of herself. With intact self-worth and confidence, she knew that David wasn't a good fit for her. She didn't feel threatened by his insults or his frequent efforts to control her.

Caring for Your Inner Child

A hard-hitting reality that came crashing down on me when I discovered the importance of understanding your inner child is that *as long as those childhood problems aren't resolved, you will continue to be vulnerable to abuse.*

It's difficult to attract someone who *isn't* a narcissist if you're still struggling with the same issues from your younger years because they maintain your need for *dependence, acceptance, and validity.* They keep you *fearful of abandonment and rejection* which are an abuser's favorite things to exploit.

That said, it's important that you take time to care for your inner child. Yes, there is no way to change the past, and some abuse might be too adverse to truly resolve this late in life. But making an effort to minimize the damage can help you become less prone to abuse later on.

Identifying Childhood Pain

Some abusive childhood experiences can be exceptionally profound and easy to detect, like sexual abuse, verbal abuse, physical abuse and violence, or deliberate neglect. Anything your parent might have done with the malicious intent to hurt, degrade, or punish you for no apparent reason are all possible roots of adult psychological issues.

Then there are some that aren't as overt, like my experiences. Parents who don't necessarily want to inflict pain on their children but end up doing just that because of the circumstances they're forced into can also cause psychological damage, albeit far less pronounced.

Figuring out where your childhood pain stems from will make it possible for you to see how they manifest now that you're an adult. For example, a girl who was frequently ridiculed by her mother for her eating habits might manifest eating disorders later in life. Women who are sexually abused as children are likely to struggle with body image issues, emotional instability, and intimacy limitations.

If you're having a hard time figuring out where your adult issues are stemming from, you can examine yourself in reverse. Pick out the issues you see yourself struggling with presently, and then try to tie them into an experience you had as a child.

For example, Claire noticed that she was struggling with openness. She was always on the defensive and found it very difficult to let anyone into her life. Aside from what she allowed her friends to see on the surface, there wasn't a lot that anyone else knew about her because she was very careful to share anything on a more personal level.

Claire examined herself and tried to figure out why she was being so closed off. When she dug deeper, she came to discover that her guarded personality was stemming from the fact that she was frequently shamed as a child for speaking up about her feelings or for being too opinionated.

After having been regularly shot down by her parents for the things she would share, Claire developed a recluse persona. This helped her avoid the shame and criticism that she feared she would receive in her adult years, since that's what she experienced as a child.

Reparenting Your Inner Child

Again, I'd like to reiterate that there likely isn't anything inherently wrong with the way your parents raised you. In fact, they may have had very good intentions when they made the parenting decisions they chose. But because we're all prone to remiss and error, it's only likely that they might have not been able to fully meet your childhood needs.

While it would be possible to communicate these issues with your parents now, there's really very little they can offer you in order to reconcile the mistakes they made in the past - especially if they were as seemingly harmless as those I experienced.

Ultimately, at this point in your life, it's ideal that you *seek and adopt* your wounded inner child. This small child needs to feel love, security, and a sense of stability that no one else can provide except yourself - because you are best equipped to provide your inner child with the unconditional affection that you might need.

Now, how exactly do you go about healing this wounded child? It's really simple - as long as you know where the fault lies. In Claire's case, it's simply a matter of seeking out a safe, guilt-free avenue where she can express her feelings, opinions, and thoughts without judgement. Allowing herself to do what her childhood self could only dream of doing will free her from that pain and re-establish the confidence to share herself with the world.

In more serious cases of abuse, it's often recommended that you seek out professional help and enroll yourself in group therapy sessions to help you process your anger and pain. Yes, the road to recovery can be long and frightening, but taking those first few steps into healing can make it possible for you to heal the wounded child you once were.

Engaging Your Inner Child

It's possible to re-parent your inner child by engaging her through meditation and visualization. Of course, you already know how much writing has helped me with my healing, which is why I once again recommend that you try a few writing exercises to help you engage your inner child.

Try performing these exercises and answering the questions that follow:

Find a picture of yourself as a child. Imagine that child playing, studying, or going about her day with you in the background as a silent onlooker. This first step will help establish the reality of your childhood and make it easier to connect with your inner child as you go along.

Now, try to remember in as much detail as possible one of the most memorable moments you had as a child. It can help to write things down.

What part of the experience made it memorable to you? How did you feel being a child witnessing or living through that specific event?

What did you love most about your parents?

Would you describe them as supportive, loving, and affectionate? Why or why not?

What did you dislike about growing up in your family? Was there favoritism? Did your parents have specific parenting techniques that you didn't like? Go in as much detail as possible.

If there's something you could change about the way you grew up, what would it be and why?

Chapter 5 - Creating Your Own Thoughts

A major goal you should set out to accomplish once you free yourself from the clutches of a narcissist is to *re-establish your independence and individuality*. Your abuser *took control from you, made you doubt yourself,* and *forced you to submit your thoughts, feelings, and actions* to him. So, you might now feel confused when it comes to thinking without the puppeteer's strings telling you where to steer your mind.

But as I learned through the course of my own healing, *regaining control is important* not only because it puts your best interest as the primary concern, but also because it limits your vulnerability to another narcissistic partner.

Victims who are left hanging, who fail to recover, who don't take control of their thoughts after the destruction of a narcissistic partner might still look for someone to *control them*. This pathological neediness and dependence will continue to seek someone who will take the reins because the victim is *still afraid to make decisions on her own*.

Aiming to re-establish that sense of self-confidence - that YOU know what's best for yourself - will keep you from engaging with someone who doesn't have your best interest in mind.

5 Steps to Regain Control

How exactly to you rewire your brain from seeking external approval to accepting internal direction? No doubt, becoming self-sufficient and independent after narcissistic abuse can be difficult - but it's not impossible. Here are a few doable steps you can take to help you regain control of your thoughts.

Get Rid of the Poor Self-Concept

Before anything else, you need to rid yourself of the poor self-concept. What do I mean? I mean don't try to move through the healing process with your thoughts dictating or limiting *who you are. "I'm just naturally anxious", "I've always been lacking in confidence", "I never really learned how to be fully independent."* **Stop**.

Branding yourself means that you've already cut any potential for change before it could even bloom and flourish. You are a human being with an incredible capacity to change and improve, so don't think for one second that the *way you've been will prevent you from ever becoming anything else.*

You can change for the better, and it's possible for you to destroy even some of the oldest personality traits you've been living with - all it takes is effort, diligence, and dedication.

Refocus Your Mind

What do you usually think about when you're lying awake in bed at night? Do you linger on the pain? Do you think about the instances when your ex's narcissistic tendencies shined through, but you were just too caught up to recognize them? Do you imagine what life would have been like if you hadn't fallen for him in the first place?

Should have, would have, could have. Unfortunately, no amount of rumination will change the things that happened. What you can do however, is change your future. You can start that by refocusing your mind.

Instead of thinking about what might have been, think *what could be.* Ask yourself, *what thoughts would you prefer to fill your head before you sleep at night? Do you like being worried, fearful, and in pain? Or would you rather go to bed at night with thoughts of being in control, independent, and self-sufficient?*

Simply *imagining* the kind of person you'd like to be and the kind of mental stability you'd like to have makes it possible for you to start the process of reprogramming your mind. By maintaining your focus on positive thoughts that put yourself in a good light, you can steer your mind to a better state that's easier to build on.

Developing the Habit

In the previous step, your purpose was to *train your thoughts*. Choosing to think about positive things can be a challenge, especially if you're hurting. But if you successfully complete this step, you can move on to the next which involves developing the habits of the person you want to be.

Now that you're thinking more like a confident, independent, and responsible individual, it's time that you establish the habits that one might possess. This works by seeking out opportunities throughout your day and being mindful of your reactions.

- When you encounter an inconvenience, such as missing the train on the way to work, how would your well-rounded version respond?

- If a coworker pushes your buttons while you're working your shift, what's the responsible, mature way to respond?

- You're on your way home from work and you're confronted with insane traffic that keeps you on the road for hours - what's the appropriate reaction?

Lots of minor inconveniences we encounter throughout the day can be opportunities for us to practice *the new versions of ourselves*. Exercising this deliberate control of our actions daily helps condition our minds and gives your brain a more precise idea of how you want it to respond.

Soon enough, the process will become *effortless* and you'll start to act and think the way you've conditioned yourself to without having to put in any conscious effort.

Be Your Biggest Motivator

They say that breaking old habits is the hardest part of change, but I don't really think that's true. In fact, I believe that breaking old habits can be pretty easy. The hard part is making sure that old habits that have been broken *stay broken*.

Falling back into self-depreciation and criticism is something that will constantly threaten your progress. That's because the narcissist's damage can be so deeply ingrained that the abused victim in you can keep rearing its head to beat you back into your old self-concept.

I've found that *sticking to a new mental state* can be much more difficult than breaking the old one you've been conditioned to operate under. It's important to make sure that you keep motivating yourself to stay on track. Now, the question is how exactly you can do that?

- **Set the mood.** At the start of every day, take a few minutes to clear your mind. Remember the last time that you felt most confident or proud of the way you reacted or responded to an external stimulus in your day. Keep that moment in your head and try to be that person throughout your routine.

- **Make no room for negativity**. We're always quick to close ads that annoy us when we're browsing on our phones, or to mute a phone-call from a person we're just not that interested in talking to. So why should you allow unwanted thoughts to dwell in your mind? The moment that you start to generate thoughts that are critical, judgmental, or negative about yourself, make sure to shut them out and clear them away. Always focus on the person *you want to be* and make no room for self-criticism.

- **Envision your triumph**. Right before you go to bed, avoid thinking about all the things that went wrong throughout the day, or the minute changes you should have made to your reactions and responses. Those moments are long gone. Instead, try to imagine tomorrow. Envision going through the entire day as the person you want to be. This will make it easier to wake up with the kind of mentality that will help you move towards your goal.

Keep Your Emergency Kit at the Ready

When I was going through the process of regaining control of my thoughts, I would often find myself feeling stuck. For instance, one of my goals was to become less critical of my financial decisions, but there were times that I would just freeze when confronted with the need to purchase *anything*.

In those moments, I would feel completely powerless and start to feel anxious. *My new self was falling apart.* Now, because this happened quite a few times, I thought it would be important to develop a psychological emergency kit that granted me access to some important techniques I could use to help reestablish my goals in those unanticipated moments.

- **Deep breathing**. As one of the simplest relaxation techniques, deep breathing is a strategy that's incorporated into a lot of therapies and psychotherapies because it's an effective method for releasing tension. I found that deep breathing 5 times could significantly relieve the stress and anxiety I was feeling allowing me to refocus myself on positive thoughts.

- **Limbering up**. Movement is a great way to release negative energies. Stretching, jumping in place, or jogging up and down a hallway for a few seconds really helped save me from those moments of hopelessness to reestablish my goals.

- **Repeating a mantra**. Think of a short, sweet, positive saying that you can use to refuel your efforts. Something along the lines of "I'm doing great!" or "I can do this!" are great examples of mantras you can repeat to yourself to reprogram your mind and erase negative thoughts and feelings that might pop up.

- **Indulging in a treat**. One of the ways that I healed my inner child was by offering myself a piece of chocolate whenever I felt I did something right. After a while, I started to associate chocolate with all the good things, I became a better person.

As a part of my emergency kit, I would indulge in one piece during the most challenging parts of reprogramming my thoughts. This would help me focus on all the good I've done to get to where I am, making the minor issue of the present seem much smaller and insignificant.

Keep in mind that everyone has different preferences when it comes to reestablishing the feeling of positivity after a minor slip-up. Try to understand yourself and how you react to setbacks, then choose the best tools to help you effectively curb a down moment to get yourself back on track as soon as possible.

The Value of Mindfulness

In this part of the process, you will learn to appreciate the value of mindfulness. As one of the concepts of meditation, mindfulness involves developing a heightened awareness of your present situation. This helps you shut out negativity as it happens and makes it possible for victims to break learned patterns that might have become *automatic* as the result of abuse.

For instance, my first reaction when confronted with negative criticism was to clam up and say sorry. It was something I learned to do after discovering my ex's critical nature. Now that our relationship is over, it's possible that I might still receive criticism from people in my life - especially my friends and family.

Unfortunately, I found that I would react the same way in the face of constructive criticism, because I was conditioned to think that *all criticism* was derogatory and painful.

It took mindfulness and awareness to be able to combat that automatic behavior. So, I had to put in a conscious effort to make sure I didn't just bow out and apologize, especially if that wasn't the most appropriate response to what I was being told.

Often, victims will navigate the world on auto-pilot. Shutting out stimulation and keeping your emotions out of the loop makes it easier to get through daily life because you get to shield yourself from possible pain and insult. So, a lot of the things you might do may be programmed - automatic and effortless on your end.

Practicing mindfulness will help make you aware of these automatic reactions and responses you may have learned, giving you the opportunity to change them and become better adjusted to act on external stimulation *individually* instead of in a generalized way.

Tips for Improving Mindfulness

- **Time away**. An effective mindfulness improvement method that really worked for me was getting time away. Busy city streets, the daily grind, and lots of other distractions and noise can eat up your mental bandwidth and divide your attention. Spending some time away from it all regularly can help you tap into your awareness and centralize your focus.

    You don't need to pay for an expensive getaway trip to a remote island in the Pacific to be able to give yourself some quiet time. A walk in the park, a quiet dinner alone, or just a long drive through a less populated area of your locality can all be great ways to remove yourself from the daily hustle and bustle.

- **Meditation**. Of course, as one of the cornerstones of meditation, mindfulness can be practiced through meditation. Find a quiet place to sit, and make sure you have a few minutes to spare without any potential distractions interrupting your practice.

Close your eyes and count backwards from 10 slowly. With each number, release tension and apprehension and try to clear your mind from any stress that might be eating you up. As you reach 1, take a deep breath and release it slowly, feeling the air as it exits your lungs.

Now, instead of trying to empty your mind, allow ideas and thoughts to come as they do. Examine them one by one before releasing them shortly after. Try not to think of anything for too long.

After a few minutes of this, count slowly from 1 to 10, inhale deeply and then release the breath slowly. Open your eyes and maintain silence for a few seconds before concluding your practice.

- **Mindfulness in action.** Try to look for a TV show or movie that would encourage you to react or respond to the events they present. Crime and drama shows are great places to start.

  As you watch, try to keep track of how your mind thinks. *What is your typical thought response to the events depicted? Are you responding in an appropriate way, like a well-rounded person would? Or are there better ways for you to react?*

  Continue to shape your thought process and end ideas and concepts if they're not aligned with your concept of what's right and appropriate. Make sure to stay on top of your thoughts as you watch to help make accurate adjustments when they're necessary.

How to Affirm Yourself

Self-affirmation is a powerful tool for strengthening your confidence and sense of self-worth. These short phrases help you improve your mindset and get rid of unwanted negative self-concepts that could be keeping you from your goal to control your own thoughts.

You probably don't know it, but you might already have a few affirmative thoughts that you tell yourself daily - just not the kind that will help you become the person you want to be.

Here are some of the most common thoughts of affirmation I've encountered in my journey to help women overcome emotional abuse:

- I'll never find love again.

- Bad things always happen to me.

- Everyone leaves me.

- It would take a miracle for me to lose weight.

- I never could stick to anything that I promised to be faithful to.

These "mantras" that you might unconsciously tell yourself can severely damage your progress and keep you from living your best possible life. So instead of sticking to them, it would be in your best interest to break the bad thoughts and develop *new, more positive phrases for self-affirmation that you can repeat to yourself when life gets you down.*

Here are a few steps to developing your new affirmative phrase:

1. Start your affirmative phrase with the words "*I am...*"
2. Keep it *positive,* so avoid using words like not or never. Phrases stated with a positive tone have a much more powerful effect to them, since they're perceived to be more proactive instead of limiting or restrictive.
3. Think of what you want to *become.* Be specific.
4. Use an action word in the present tense and try to keep your statement dynamic.
5. Don't get too wordy - just say what you want to say minus all the fancy bells and whistles.

Here's an example of an affirmative statement that you might come up with using these guidelines:

"*I am proud of myself for my continuing progression into self-discovery and independence.*"

Or something like, "*I am grateful to be making decisions on *my own now - completely in charge of the rewards and consequences."*

Now, if you come face to face with a drawback or if something just doesn't go your way, instead of repeating your old affirmative phrase to yourself, you can use your new one. Deflecting any negativity with your own breed of positivity will make it easier for you to jump back on your horse and move on through the challenges.

Chapter 6 - Survivor Mode

During the *victim mode* of the healing phase, most of your effort will be directed towards managing pain, anger, and other strong emotions that you might have felt as a result of the abuse. In the latter part of the first phase, you should have also started rewiring your thought process to start breaking down the shackles that the narcissist might have set in place in your mind.

Now, I'd like to congratulate you for getting this far - you're through the first phase! In this second phase called *survivor mode*, we're going to focus more on *yourself* instead of the emotions and feelings that might have been left behind from your breakup.

At this point, I remember that I had to shift my focus from trying to address the pain, anger, and betrayal, and instead rebuilding my life. I wanted to move *past* the abuse and become a new person free from that experience. I didn't want my days to be *all about my narcissistic ex*, so I had to recharge and refocus my energy on *myself*.

During the survivor phase, you might have one or more of these thoughts:

- I'm not ready to forgive yet
- I want to become my own person again

- I want to live life without the shackles of abuse

- I'm not always angry anymore, but memories may bring those negative feelings back to the surface

- I still deal with triggers that either hinder my progress or make me feel like I'm back to square one

- I'm having a hard time believing that not everyone is a narcissist

You might not feel the emotions as profoundly as you did at the start and you may actually have a few good days that go by without any memories of your abuse. But certain moments, events, and triggers can easily bring negative memories and feelings back to the surface in a heartbeat, and these can make you feel like you're reliving the experience all over again.

Don't worry - it's normal. Anyone who has ever made a complete recovery from the damage of narcissistic abuse probably went through the same thing. I'm sure I did. What's important is that you keep your eyes on the prize, and you forgive *yourself* for the times when you might not be able to stay on track as you had planned.

Is It PTSD?

In a lot of ways, you might think that your situation resembles post-traumatic stress disorder. PTSD is a mental health condition in which an individual might feel profound fear, anxiety, or stress when triggered by a traumatic event they lived through or witnessed. For instance, some of the most common individuals affected by PTSD are soldiers who survived war.

Of course, narcissistic abuse isn't anything compared to war, but you must realize that different people have specific vulnerabilities. For example, one person might cope better with emotional abuse, are able to simply walk away and move on no matter how bad they might have been treated because they're better equipped to deal with the trauma. Put another person in that situation, and they might be completely torn up for years afterwards.

Remember - we all grew up differently. So, someone who was parented properly, who was given the ideal tools to be able to efficiently cope with emotional abuse, who was brought up feeling secure and confident in their capabilities might be less affected by emotional trauma. Those who weren't lucky enough to get that kind of foundation might be particularly traumatized.

So, is it possible to develop PTSD after an emotionally abusive, narcissistic relationship? *Yes, it is, as long as you experienced enough trauma to be able to fit the criteria for PTSD.*

How Can You Tell if You Have PTSD?

There are specific qualifiers and standardized criteria that specialists use to diagnose PTSD. If you suspect that you might be suffering from PTSD, it's recommended that you seek the advice of a mental health specialist in order to get the appropriate treatment.

How can you tell if you *might* be suffering from PTSD in the first place? Consider these factors:

- You have unwanted, intrusive memories of the abusive relationship that make you feel profoundly unsafe, fearful, or anxious.

- When confronted with memories of the relationship, you feel like you're there again, reliving the experience.

- Physical manifestations of stress and anxiety such as sweating, increased heart rate, or heavy breathing, when dealing with memories of the relationship or talking about the experience.

- Putting significant effort into trying to avoid ideas and thoughts concerning the experience.

- Deliberately avoiding places, people, or activities that might be closely associated with your abusive relationship.

- Generalized hopelessness, thinking that the world is a bad place and there is no possibility of improvement.

- Decreased interest and engagement in activities that you might have once enjoyed.

- Withdrawal from family and friends.

- Gaps in your memory, even if they didn't have anything to do with the traumatic event.

- Complete emotional shutdown.

- Destructive or possibly harmful behavior such as alcohol and drug abuse.

- Difficulty concentrating and sleeping.

Getting Help

If you suspect that you might have PTSD, it's imperative that you receive prompt treatment. PTSD can be a life-threatening condition and may significantly impair your occupational and social functioning. So, try to get assistance and medical attention as soon as possible.

Where can you go to get help for PTSD or similar mental health issues?

1. **Enroll in therapy classes**. Mental health therapy sessions can be a great avenue for releasing negative memories. Here, you can talk to specialists and other individuals who might have gone through similar experiences. At first, I was reluctant to enroll in therapy because I felt like there was a stigma surrounding the process.

> *I didn't want to be branded that way.* But it's important to remember that your experiences do *not define you.* You're simply a person trying to discover healing, so don't think that anything you do towards that goal will label you negatively.
>
> If you're not ready to enroll in a class just yet, you can try seeking out online forums or internet-based coaching for PTSD or emotionally abusive relationships. These courses can offer you training and related exercises to help you process the trauma and make your way to a full recovery.

2. **Get out**. PTSD will force you to stay indoors, to avoid interactions with anyone at all costs, to isolate yourself and try to escape the world outside. Isn't it just horrible how after surviving a traumatic relationship, you'd be forced to be *alone* because of the severe mental and emotional damage you sustain?

> While I know it's tough to break through the chains, *you* are the only one who can truly fight the impulse to be held back by your pain. *Do you want to gratify*

the trauma by letting it isolate you? Or do you want to be in control of your own life?

Instead of staying indoors and avoiding people, try getting out more. You don't have to visit the club, the bar, or other densely populated, lively areas right off the bat. You can start small. Personally, I made a conscious effort to visit my parents more often. I went to their house over the weekend and stayed with them overnight. I would take the time to catch up and tried to make sure I opened up a little more with each visit.

Later, I found myself reconnecting with friends. We would have brunches together and go on short trips to the mall. Sometimes, when I felt particularly unmotivated, I would just go out to the park and people-watch. It wasn't interaction, sure. But it was better than staying indoors for days, sulking in my pain and trauma.

3. **Focus on the positives**. Too often, we're left fixating our gaze on how horrible life has become. We feel hopeless, insignificant, and unhappy about where we are and what has happened to our lives. But I want you to remember that often, there are countless wonderful occurrences and little miracles that happen throughout our day that we fail to see because we *choose* to look at all the negatives.

One of the most powerful things you'll ever learn to do throughout your healing experience is *choose where to focus your energy*. Instead of thinking of how everything went wrong, *choose* to think of all the little positives you experience. Doing this will slowly but surely recalibrate your mind to ignore bad things and be grateful for the positives in your life.

Gratitude Exercises

Developing a grateful attitude can be a slow process especially if you're coming from a place of trauma and hurt. So, it would help to write things down to solidify your thought processes.

Here are a few writing exercises to help with your improvement:

1. ***Think about yesterday.*** Can you list a minimum of 5 instances when you felt lucky, happy, or thankful? It can be as grand as receiving a promotion or as simple as getting a free coffee to go with your breakfast meal.

2. ***Is there a special person in your life who has been instrumental in your healing?*** Write a private letter of gratitude to tell this person how they've helped you recover. You have the option to keep the letter to yourself or to send it their way.

3. ***When was the last time someone thanked you***

for something you did? It could be a complete stranger or a close relative or friend. How did it make you feel to be on the receiving end of their gratitude?

4. ***What specific aspects of your life are you most thankful for?*** Are you happy to have your family and friends, your job, and your home? In what ways do these aspects make your life fulfilling and worthwhile?

5. ***What experiences have you had in the past 2 years that you feel significantly grateful for?*** How did these events shape you to become the person you are today?

Chapter 7 - Thriving Mode

When I started out my recovery journey, I was honestly skeptical the whole time. I felt so low, fearful, and anxious - how could I possibly turn my life around if I was coming from such a horrible experience? Fortunately, with lots of determination, effort, and the help of loving people and therapeutic communities around me, I was able to move past the trauma and recover completely from my experience.

I want you to know that *you can have that, too. All the things that are stopping you from healing are* **inside your head**. Once you work through them, change those thoughts, and develop a new way of thinking, *you can set yourself free.*

You don't need to wait **for anyone to save you** - YOU are fully capable of saving yourself! You just need to believe that you can.

At this point, you might be wondering - *how long will it take for me to feel completely free from the experience?* Right now, I must be honest with you. There is no way to accurately measure the time it will take for you to feel secure, happy, and independent once again. **It's different for everyone.**

Just as your unique childhood could hasten or impede your progress, your **unique recovery journey** could also affect the rate at which you heal. No two people are the same - but what I can guarantee is that **everyone can heal**.

Building Self-Confidence

When I was released from my abusive relationship, I discovered that my *confidence* was one of the most severely damaged aspects of my personality. I couldn't make decisions on my own, I was always second guessing myself, and I couldn't bring myself to face anyone thinking they could see right through me and into my trauma.

It was a tough start to rediscover my confidence, but it was an *essential* part of regaining control of my own thoughts. Without the self-doubt, the constant questioning, the endless going back-and-forth wondering whether I was doing the right thing, I was able to become an efficient, self-sustaining adult once more.

How to Re-Establish Confidence

1. **Love Yourself.** A lack of self-confidence ties in closely to your sense of self-worth. Your narcissistic ex had to make sure to break down your self-esteem because it would help make you more dependent on him. The more you would depend on him, the more control he would have over you.

So, the first step to recovering your confidence is to re-establish your self-esteem. How exactly can you do that? Taking baby steps towards rekindling self-worth is often ideal because it uncomplicates the process, dividing the journey into doable chunks.

Start a new diet, enroll in fitness classes, take regular bubble baths, treat yourself to a massage at least once a week - whatever you think qualifies as *self-care* is a great place to start building your self-esteem. Think of activities that are given typically to VIPs. By engaging in these kinds of experiences, you teach yourself that you *deserve good treatment because you're worth it.*

2. **Talk to yourself**. Who better to give you a pep talk than yourself? At the beginning, it can be tough to get out of your shell and seek interaction with other people. So, don't think that you have to *force yourself* into an uncomfortable situation. In fact, attempting to push yourself to talk to others now could be detrimental to your confidence especially if the interaction doesn't go how you thought it would.

So instead of trying to exercise your budding confidence in front of others, try it out for yourself first. Stand in front of a mirror, look at yourself, and just start talking. You can pretend that you're talking to a friend or a new acquaintance, but it often works best if you try to talk to *yourself*.

Tell yourself all the positive things that have

happened since leaving your relationship and starting your journey to self-discovery. Formulate a strategy on how you intend to go about your day and reinforce your mindset by telling yourself one of your affirmative phrases (which you formulated in an earlier chapter).

Do this regularly, and once you feel comfortable, you'll start to feel a stronger *presence* when faced with new people or old friends and acquaintances.

3. **One day at a time.** Disappointment is easy to feel if you're coming from a defeated experience. You feel used, tired, and helpless, and you're probably thinking your efforts aren't really going to take you anywhere - you're just doing it for the sake of trying.

With this kind of mentality, any minor slip-up or drawback can make you feel completely disappointed in yourself. So, the best way to avoid it would be to *stop setting unattainable or impossible goals.*

Failure becomes inevitable when you set goals that aren't realistic. Most people think they can achieve monumental change in a few weeks' time and aim to accomplish large hurdles towards improvement. *You don't need to do that.*

Just like the proverbial tortoise that went up against a hare, you need to remember that *slow and steady* is always better. This isn't a race, and you aren't in a competition with anyone. You won't lose the chance to redeem yourself if you don't do it fast enough. *Time is not running out.* Try to avoid setting goals that put you in a position of failure.

Instead of setting such big goals that you tell yourself to achieve over a short period of time, choose to set smaller goals. Little things like trying to wake up a little earlier than usual, sending a message to a friend you haven't talked to in a while, or trying a new recipe might all seem like they have *nothing* to do with your confidence. But over time, an accumulation of these small positive acts can have a massive impact on how you feel about yourself.

Goal for Gold - Writing Exercises for Goal Setting

The way you formulate your goals and decide on their pace will greatly affect how often you slip-up and how effectively you move though the process of improvement. It's imperative that you know how to set realistic goals that won't be *too* unattainable.

Here's how you can visualize the right goals:

1. **Imagine the perfect day**. Think of yourself as the person you want to be. What would the typical perfect day be for a person like that? Here are some factors to consider:

- What time would you wake up? What would you do as soon as you got out of bed?

- Would there be any sort of ritual that you'd do in the morning? Like meditation or prayer?

- How does the morning self-care routine look?

- Once you step out the door, how do you interact with the people you come across?

- At work, what are the attitudes and behaviors you adapt to make sure that your tasks are accomplished efficiently and perfectly?

- Do you go home immediately after work? Or do you stop by a place to meet with friends and enjoy some company?

- What does your after-work self-care routine look like?

- Before you get to bed, what do you do to sign-off from the day?

2. **Pick out discrepancies**. Now that you know what the *ideal* perfect day looks like, you can see how it differs from the way you're currently spending your days. *What are the differences you saw in the way your ideal self dealt with daily life compared to the way you've been doing it thus far?*

Picking out the discrepancies will help you decide how to

set your goals. For instance, if your *ideal self* would make sure to spend at least 30-minutes on a skin-care routine every morning, but that's not something you're already doing, *that can be one of your primary goals.*

Seeing where the differences lie will make it easier to augment your current routine and situation, so it resembles your ideal life more accurately. These small changes might seem insignificant, but they will make you feel much more confident and important as the days roll on.

3. **Set the pace**. While it's absolutely acceptable to start working with smaller goals and then working your way up to bigger ones, it's also important to make sure you're *progressing* with the goals you've set.

That said, you may want to consider graduating your goals so that you step up the ladder as the weeks, months, and years move along. For instance, you can set the goal to spend an hour at the park at least once every weekend.

After the first week of successfully visiting the park an hour at a time every Saturday, you can add another facet to your goal. Visit the park for an hour *and* say hi and give a smile to every person you come across. On the third week, you could visit the park, say hi to and smile at the people you encounter, and spark a conversation with at least one stranger.

This process of adding to previous goals maintains the challenge and keeps things from becoming monotonous. It also helps guarantee that you're *improving* and not just being stagnantly held in place by static goals.

Now that you know *which* goals are best for you, it's time to write them down. Remember, phrasing your goals the right way plays a large role in their attainability. The more appropriate your wording, the more likely you are to succeed.

1. Start with the words "I will..." This is probably the strongest phrase in the English language because it expresses certainty and resilience, and they communicate a promise to succeed.

2. Think of the discrepancies you saw in your visualization of the *perfect day*. What activities or actions should you adapt to live your ideal life? Condense that into an action phrase.

3. Add a modifier. *How* do you want to complete the goal you've set?

By following the steps above, you can come up with a goal similar to this:

"I will complete a 30-minute workout routine daily at my peak physical capacity."

Or something along the lines of, *"I will quietly enjoy a leisurely walk around my neighborhood before starting my day."*

These goals are simple, precise, and absolutely doable, because they break down every aspect of the process for you to be able to understand *fully* what you need to do in order to accomplish them.

Begin with a minimum of 3 goals and try to make sure that you're doing at least one of them every day. Make sure to add a few adjustments and facets to your routine as you become accustomed to the goals, so you can keep yourself moving towards improvement and progress.

Chapter 8 - Getting into a New Relationship

You probably thought at the start of your healing journey that you would *never want to date ever again*. I felt the same way. I was too hurt and afraid to open myself up to anyone, and I was convinced that everyone around me would be exactly like my ex.

But as you allow yourself to grow and bloom, you'll realize that love after pain is very possible. In fact, falling in love again might very well be the absolute end of the hurt you've been dealt. But of course, no one is rushing you to find a new relationship - you *don't need anyone* to make you feel complete or whole, and this entire recovery process is about *you*.

Now, the topic of *falling in love again after narcissistic abuse* can be pretty long and drawn-out, so bear with me if it gets a little complicated. I do promise though, that at the end of this chapter, you'll have better insight as to the timing and purpose of a future relationship, as well as your potential partner's viability as a suitable choice for *you*.

The Signs of Readiness

One question that I often get asked is *"How will I know if I'm ready to fall in love again?"* Unfortunately, a lot of women use their *heart* to tell whether or not *love is something they want or need at any given moment*. The sad reality is that the heart is rarely ever a reliable compass when it comes to determining the viability of a new relationship.

Keep in mind that your heart operates on *feelings*. Those fluttery butterflies in your tummy might make you think you're face to face with the right guy. But do those feelings tell you about *your readiness? Your current emotional state? Your preparedness for commitment?*

Following your heart isn't the best mantra to follow if you're seeking love again after a narcissistic relationship. Remember, the heart can be deceptive at times, and love can be very alluring - even if you've already been hurt. It's important that you know *when* you're actually ready instead of relying on the speed of your heartbeat when looking at a potential mate.

Here are some things you can ask yourself to find out whether you're ready to love again:

- Can you think about your previous, narcissistic relationship and honestly say that you're past the pain and hurt?

- Do you feel happy, content, and confident in your current situation?

- Were you able to resolve the problems of your inner child?

- Are you enjoying your new-found freedom?

- Do you feel like there's nothing you need to change in your life right now to feel *happier* or *more satisfied?*

If you answered yes to all the questions above, then you *might just be ready to find love again.* But if you said *no* to even just one of them, then you might want to consider holding off.

A woman that's ready to love again after a narcissistic relationship should be able to say that she's *free and self-*

sustaining. After all the effort you put into repairing yourself, you should be able to say that having a man in your life might be a great adventure, but it isn't necessarily an integral part of your happiness.

Processing your pain and anger, finding the roots of your vulnerability, resolving the issues of your inner child, and discovering the stronger, independent *you* will help you feel *secure* in yourself. You *won't need a man to be happy*, and you won't feel pressured to find love. If it finds you, then you'll likely welcome the opportunity.

So, what does unpreparedness look like? Here are some characteristics of a previously abused woman who might be looking for love at the wrong time:

- Hoping to fill in "gaps" or "missing pieces" in her happiness

- Operating under the idea that a man's love will "complete" or "fix" her

- Rushing into any semblance of a relationship she can find, even if she's not entirely interested in the person she's chosen

- Putting all other aspects of her life on hold until she finds a man

- Falling into short-lived relationships one after the other

One major piece of information that I always try to make clear to the women who come to me for advice on finding love again is that *your happiness should never be tied to anyone outside of yourself.* You are a **complete human being**, and you don't need a man to fix you or make you whole!

The entire purpose of the recovery journey is to make sure that you will no longer have to face that kind of trauma and abuse in the future. So yes, healing might take time. But what you can gain from the entire experience is *peace of mind* knowing that you'll make the best choices for yourself later on.

Don't skip the steps, and don't fixate your gaze on a partner! Once you're completely healed, you can make informed decisions that prevent you from becoming a narcissist's prey once more.

Redefining Sexy

Even though I don't perfectly fit my Mom's/Dad's idea of what a child should be, I can try my best to meet their standards to deserve their love!

As a child, this train of thought might have been one of the major motivators that fueled your actions. It may have manifested as an aggressive desire to do well in school, a religious effort to make sure all your chores were done, or an effortful plight to keep all your little siblings safe in your parents' absence.

Whatever it was, it's possible that the punishment set by your parents for the things you did against their will or preference made you feel that you needed to work harder to please them.

So, when they scolded you for failing an exam, you studied more. When they told you to stay in your room after you made a mess in the living room, you promised never to play with paint again. When your mother shouted at you for not eating your vegetables, you sat quietly with tears in your eyes while you tried to down every last brussels sprout on your plate.

As you got older, that same desire to *please* the person in control may have made you gravitate towards *controlling partners*. That's why you might ask yourself - *why do I find bad boys so sexy?* True enough, **most women** find the bad boy image to be oozing with sex appeal. Why? Because they can take control of you - the same way Mom and Dad did when you were little.

In a relationship with a narcissistic partner, you're probably back to your childhood disposition. Your partner wants you to act and be a certain way and promises to punish you if you if you don't act accordingly. This mechanism fuels you - *I need to deserve his love!*

So, you work extra hard to toe the line and try to be the woman he wants you to be, just like you did when you were a child trying to deserve your parents' love. As you may have already learned by now, *you don't need to do anything to deserve someone's love!* You are lovable just as you are. If anyone thinks you need to change in order to be loved, then perhaps you'd be better off without that person in your life.

At this point, I want to bring light to a widespread concept that we rarely ever truly understand. *True love is unconditional* because love is a choice. **It's a decision to keep loving a person even when they're being difficult to love. Love doesn't demand change - it accepts flaws.**

All of that said, it's about time you *redefine* what attracts you. No more controlling men who want to change you and turn you into their *"ideal" woman.* No more abusive narcissists who will eat you up and spit you out feeling worthless and used. No more traumatic relationships that will require years of recovery before you're *you* again.

How do you redefine sexy? No amount of visualizing or imagination can make a difference. Redefining sexy relies on your effort to resolve your inner child's issues. That's why we talked about it a few chapters back!

Learning to feel attracted to a new breed of man requires that you erase what attracts you to them in the first place. Another thing I've noticed is that women who have resolved internal issues concerning their childhood don't *actively* seek out a partner.

They *attract* well-rounded men because these people can sense a stable woman. And a responsible, smart, and healthy male partner will *want* to establish a relationship with a similar woman because he values stability - the idea that they love each other, but don't necessarily *need* each other to feel happy and content.

Becoming Your Own Happiness

If there's one thing I want you to remember after all of this has been said and done, is that you are *responsible for your own happiness*. You don't need a man's love, you don't need anyone else but *yourself* to feel truly joyful. Once you discover that and find happiness without the need for external affection, acceptance, and validation, you can build a healthy relationship with the *right* person.

In essence, all the steps, exercises, and tips I've shared in previous chapters all have one goal - to make you feel secure and content in *who you are*. To help you develop a strong sense of independent self-worth - that you *deserve love* even when there isn't a man giving it to you.

In a lot of ways, loving yourself ties closely to loving life. The more you enjoy your *single life* the easier it will be for you to realize that you don't really need a man to feel complete. Life can be complete even if you're on your own, and a romantic partnership isn't all there is for you to yearn for or seek.

As you continue through your healing journey, take the time to *enjoy each day*. Look for moments in every day that you can smile about and be thankful for. Engage in new activities, discover new hobbies, talk with old friends and make new ones, spend time with family, care for yourself, splurge on a vacation - do the things that make *you* happy. And you'll find yourself living the life of your dreams, without the need for a man by your side.

Single and Blessed

What if you reach a point in your life where you feel that engaging in a romantic relationship with a man might be detrimental to the current happiness and contentment that you're enjoying? Do you *need* to have a boyfriend, partner, or husband even if you feel like you'd be better off without one?

Although I completely understand how you might feel that you don't need a man *at all*, especially if you really took the time to pamper yourself, it's important to know that in some cases, an aversion to men can also be a problem. Escaping or avoiding romantic relationships could be a sign of another deep-seated issue, probably stemming from the abuse you experienced. So, unless that's resolved, you should try to avoid any new relationships.

On the other hand, if you don't feel avoidant of men and would really just prefer to enjoy your singlehood, then that's absolutely fine. Some women find so much purpose and joy in living their lives for themselves that they feel that having a partner is completely unnecessary, and that's okay, too.

What do I recommend? Entertain love if it walks through your door. Give it a chance if you feel like you're ready, especially if your prospect seems like a well-balanced, mature individual like yourself. If it doesn't work out, there's nothing tying you down. You can walk away when it doesn't feel right - remember, *you control your life.*

Conclusion

Love. They say it's one of the most powerful forces in the world. It can build you up and tear you down in the blink of an eye. But if you use it right, it can be the strongest shield you could ever have against any form of abuse you might be put up against.

Self-love is an important part of establishing a healthy relationship, and a powerful tool against becoming a victim of abuse. Learning to be your own most passionate lover gives you a strong sense of self-worth and confidence. In learning to believe in your inherent value as a human being, you become more aggressive against attacks to your person.

Yes, it might have been painful. You might have felt hopeless. You were probably on the brink of giving up. *But you didn't.* The mere fact that you went through this guide with me *means that you know there's something worth saving.*

The fact that you took the time to learn about yourself, to discover techniques to rediscover who you are after abuse, to nurse that wounded inner child inside means that *you do hope, you do believe, and you do want to live your best life.*

I hope that by sharing my experiences, you were able to learn a thing or two about what you can do to become the best version of yourself *for yourself.* I know, it's not easy, and the urge to give up might feel overwhelming at times.

But don't let defeat kick you out of the race. Don't let those negative feelings maintain their grip on your thoughts. *Don't let the enemy win.* The abuse is in the past - it's over. *But you're still here, and you are capable of so much.*

To help enrich your recovery experience, I recommend that you check out *What's Up?* and *Pacifica* - two brilliant anxiety management and mindfulness apps really helped me maximize the effort I put into minimizing the effects of mental and emotional stress.

Finally, I want to say *thank you*. Thank you for loving yourself enough to read this book. Thank you for trusting me to help you through your journey. And thank you for giving yourself the chance to flourish after the trauma. The world *needs* more beautiful people like you, but don't let that fuel you.

At the end of the day, your own happiness and contentment should be the only motivation you need.

Light and love.

INDEX

Personal Recovery Journal

You know how passionately I believe in *writing* as an effective tool against anxiety, stress, fear, and pain. Every time I held a pen in my hands during recovery, I would never know what wonderful truths I would learn about myself! It was always spontaneous and freeing, and I hope you feel the same way about it as I do.

To help enhance your healing, I'm sharing this 30-day recovery journal with you. All you need to do is answer the questions one day at a time and be as truthful about each one as possible.

Day 1

How do you feel today? What specific emotions are occupying most of your thoughts? Is there anything that's causing you particular distress? What is it and why do you think it's causing you stress?

Day 2

Do you know why you might have allowed yourself to fall and stay in a relationship with an abuser? How do you think this ties in to your childhood problems or traumas?

Write a short letter to your inner child to tell her how you plan to make her feel better about her issues.

Day 3

Draw an image of a woman. Can you describe how your drawing is dressed, how she's positioned, and what she might be feeling? What could she be thinking?

If you could tell her something to possibly improve her status, or if you could ask her something to help you become more like her, what would it be?

Day 4

Today is about your anger. While it's important to maintain focus on the positives, it's equally essential that you process negative feelings, so you can let them go instead of burying them deep in your thoughts.

Think of all the people who make you feel angry, upset, or unhappy, and write each one of them a 2 to 3 sentence letter telling them anything you want to say.

Day 5

If you could be anywhere in the world right now, where would you want to be? Who do you want with you and what would you do together? Do you think you could be just as happy if you were there alone? Why or why not?

Day 6

Draw your childhood home and label each room with the feelings you most closely associate with those spaces. Why do you think you feel that way about these rooms? Do you think it could have anything to do with the person you would usually find there? How so?

Day 7

When was the last time you felt happy and carefree? What do you think you can do today to reach that level of happiness again?

Day 8

Compile a list of all the negative, hurtful things that you've been told about yourself, or that you've used against yourself. Read each one and try to process them. Do you think there's any truth to them? Why or why not?

Day 9

You are what you believe yourself to be. Take yesterday's list and beside each item, write a positive, loving statement to counteract what the negative points say. Read each one and try to process them.

Are these more accurate representations of who you are? What can you do to make sure you use these statements to describe yourself from now on instead of the negative concepts from yesterday?

Day 10

If you could talk to your younger self, what would you tell her? Write a short letter saying all the things you wish you had been told as a young child.

Day 11

Is there a part of your body that you're particularly critical of? Why? Think of all the other women in your life - is this something that you think concerns them about themselves as well? Why or why not?

Day 12

Were you ever labeled something as a child, teen, or adult? Did you generally accept this branding? Do you think it accurately represents you? Why or why not? If you could give yourself your own label, what would it be and why?

Day 13

Write a story about your childhood from the third-person - it could be your first day of elementary school, your first camp out with friends, or your first public performance. Read it to yourself when you're done.

How do you feel about the story? How do you feel about your younger self?

Day 14

Today, try to imagine yourself as a child again. Then imagine an adult woman who might look sad, defeated, and lonely. What do you think your inner child would say to someone who looked that way?

Day 15

Write a letter to your future self. What do you wish for her? What do you want her to be like? What current personality traits and characteristics do you possess that you want her to forget and replace?

Day 16

Draw an image of a woman. How is she dressed? What's her posture like? What do you think she's thinking? Does she look happier and healthier compared to the woman you drew on Day 3? How so?

Day 17

Think of someone who has significantly hurt you. Now, write a letter to them describing exactly how they made you feel. Read the letter aloud and process what you wrote. Were you speaking the truth? Did you try to hurt them back with your words? In what ways can you make the letter more objective?

Day 18

Is there anyone in your life who you haven't talked to in a while that you want to reconnect with? What's keeping you from reaching out to them? If you could talk to them now, what would you say?

Day 19

How are you feeling today? If there was one thing you could change about your disposition yesterday, what would it be and why?

Day 20

Imagine yourself all dolled up and dressed in your best. What time of day is it? Where are you going? Who are you going to be with?

Day 21

Think of someone who you might have hurt. In what way did you cause them pain? Did you mean to do it? If you could write them an apology letter, what would it say?

Day 22

Think of 5 physical features you have that you feel are an asset to you. What do you like about these features?

Day 23

You are a wonderful, lovable person. What characteristics or personality traits do you think make you unique and interesting? How do they help you leave a lasting positive impression on the people around you?

Day 24

What do you consider to be your strengths? Name at least 3 and try to be specific about the times when these strengths manifested in your personal life or work life.

Day 25

Who is your celebrity idol? What is it about him/her that makes you particularly fond of them? If you could talk to him/her, what would you say?

Day 26

What was the last thing you purchased for yourself? Was it a necessity or a luxury? If you had an infinite amount of money right now, what would you spend it on and why?

Day 27

How are you feeling today? Write 5 instances from the past week when you might have exceeded your own expectations in some way. How did it make you feel to outdo your own standards?

Day 28

Life is a party! If you could throw a party right now, who would you invite? What would you be celebrating? What kind of party would it be?

Day 29

Where do you see yourself 5 years from now? Where were you 5 years ago? Are you happy with the way your life has progressed? Why or why not? What can you do to reach your 5-year goals?

Day 30

Look back at what you wrote on Day 15. Is there a difference in who you are now compared to who you were then? What changes and improvements have you made to become the future self you were addressing on that day?

Other Exercises

Here you'll find an index of all the other exercises included in the book. You can try them out while you read the chapters they belong to, or you can perform them as stand-alone exercises - there really is no rule!

Journal Writing Exercises

When we write, we often let go of our inhibitions and share deep-seated emotions that might not have surfaced through mere conversation. Thus, jotting them down can bring hidden feelings to light, allowing you to truly understand your own situation and how to deal with the damage that you've been dealt.

To start off your journal writing practice, consider answering one or two of these questions daily.

What are some of the qualities that you expect or prefer to see in an ideal partner? In what ways did your ex meet these expectations, and in what ways did they fail?

How do you feel about your current situation? Are you still fearful that your ex might be able to control you in some way? What do you think it would take for you to feel completely safe?

Who are the people in your support group? How do they fulfill your needs in terms of comfort and reassurance? Do you feel that there's anything else you could need to help improve the support you're receiving?

Where do you see yourself 5 years from now in terms of your emotional recovery? What do you think you need to do in order to fulfill that goal?

Begin Self-Discovery

Possibly the most important and helpful thing you can do to release yourself from your pseudo personality is to begin your journey to self-discovery. I know, it sounds obscure. But there are some very doable and realistic steps you can take to help rediscover who you really are.

One way that really helped me was by starting a *self-discovery journal*. Writing exercises that allow you to uncover how you would act or decide without your subconscious taking control of your every move.

Here are a few writing exercises you can try to help you become more aware of your true self.

What makes you feel most anxious or fearful? Can you give at least 3 objective reasons why these fears are rational or realistic?

If you could be anywhere at this very moment, where would you like to be and why? Can you describe how you might spend your day at this ideal location?

When do you feel happiest? Name some activities or experiences that make you feel genuinely joyful and content.

If you had a million bucks fall into your lap right now, what would you spend it on? Try not to think about it too much and be spontaneous!

Find a picture of yourself from before your abusive relationship and describe the version of yourself in that image. Next, find a picture of yourself during the narcissistic relationship and compare your two selves. What changed?

Engaging Your Inner Child

It's possible to re-parent your inner child by engaging her through meditation and visualization. Of course, you already know how much writing has helped me with my healing, which is why I once again recommend that you try a few writing exercises to help you engage your inner child.

Try performing these exercises and answering the questions that follow:

Find a picture of yourself as a child. Imagine that child playing, studying, or going about her day with you in the background as a silent onlooker. This first step will help establish the reality of your childhood and make it easier to connect with your inner child as you go along.

Now, try to remember in as much detail as possible one of the most memorable moments you had as a child. It can help to write things down.

What part of the experience made it memorable to you? How did you feel being a child witnessing or living through that specific event?

What did you love most about your parents? Would you describe them as supportive, loving, and affectionate? Why or why not?

What did you dislike about growing up in your family? Was there favoritism? Did your parents have specific parenting techniques that you didn't like? Go into as much detail as possible.

If there's something you could change about the way you grew up, what would it be and why?

They're not aligned with your concept of what's right and appropriate. Make sure to stay on top of your thoughts as you watch to help make accurate adjustments where they're necessary.

How to Affirm Yourself

Self-affirmation is a powerful tool for strengthening your confidence and sense of self-worth. These short phrases help you improve your mindset and get rid of unwanted negative self-concepts that could be keeping you from your goal to control your own thoughts.

You probably don't know it, but you might already have a few affirmative thoughts that you tell yourself daily - just not the kind that will help you become the person you want to be.

Here are some of the most common thoughts of affirmation I've encountered in my journey to help women overcome emotional abuse:

- I'll never find love again.
- Bad things always happen to me.
- Everyone leaves me.
- It would take a miracle for me to lose weight.
- I never could stick to anything that I promised to be faithful to.

These "mantras" that you might unconsciously tell yourself can severely damage your progress and keep you from living your best possible life. So instead of sticking to them, it would be in your best interest to break the bad thoughts and develop *new, more positive phrases for self-affirmation that you can repeat to yourself when life gets you down.*

Here are a few steps to developing your new affirmative phrase:

1. Start your affirmative phrase with the words "*I am...*"

2. Keep it *positive,* so avoid using words like not or never. Phrases stated with a positive tone have a much more powerful effect to them, since they're perceived to be more proactive instead of limiting or restrictive.

3. Think of what you want to *become.* Be specific.

4. Use an action word in the present tense and try to keep your statement dynamic.

5. Don't get too wordy - just say what you want to say minus all the fancy bells and whistles.

Here's an example of an affirmative statement that you might come up with using these guidelines:

"I am proud of myself for my continuing progression into self-discovery and independence."

Or something like, *"I am grateful to be making decisions on my own now - completely in charge of the rewards and consequences."*

Now, if you come face to face with a drawback or if something just doesn't go your way, instead of repeating your old affirmative phrase to yourself, you can use your new one. Deflecting any negativity with your own breed of positivity will make it easier for you to jump back on your horse and move on through the challenges.

Writing Exercises for Goal Setting

Now that you know *which* goals are best for you, it's time to write them down. Remember, phrasing your goals the right way plays a large role in their attainability. The more appropriate your wording, the more likely you are to succeed.

1. Start with the words "I will..." This is probably the strongest phrase in the English language because it expresses certainty and resilience, and they communicate a promise to succeed.

2. Think of the discrepancies you saw in your visualization of the *perfect day*. What activities or actions should you adapt to live your ideal life? Condense that into an action phrase.

3. Add a modifier. *How* do you want to complete the goal you've set?

By following the steps above, you can come up with a goal similar to this:

"I will complete a 30-minute workout routine daily at my peak physical capacity."

Or something along the lines of, *"I will quietly enjoy a leisurely walk around my neighborhood before starting my day."*

These goals are simple, precise, and absolutely doable, because they break down every aspect of the process for you to be able to understand *fully* what you need to do in order to accomplish them.

Begin with a minimum of 3 goals and try to make sure that you're doing at least one of them every day. Make sure to add a few adjustments and facets to your routine as you become accustomed to the goals, so you can keep yourself moving towards improvement and progress.

Gratitude Exercises

Developing a grateful attitude can be a slow process especially if you're coming from a place of trauma and hurt. So, it would help to write things down to solidify your thought process progress.

Here are a few writing exercises to help with your improvement:

1. ***Think about yesterday.*** Can you list a minimum of 5 instances when you felt lucky, happy, or thankful? It can be as grand as receiving a promotion or as simple as getting a free coffee to go with your breakfast meal.

2. ***Is there a special person in your life who has been instrumental in your healing?*** Write a private letter of gratitude to tell this person how they've helped you recover. You have the option to keep the letter to yourself or to send it their way.

3. ***When was the last time someone thanked you for something you did?*** It could be a complete stranger or a close relative or friend. How did it make you feel to be on the receiving end of their gratitude?

4. ***What specific aspects of your life are you most thankful for?*** Are you happy to have your family and friends, your job, and your home? In what ways do these aspects make your life fulfilling and worthwhile?

5. ***What experiences have you had in the past 2 years that feel significantly grateful for?*** How did these events shape you to become the person you are today.

CPSIA information can be obtained
at www.ICGtesting.com
Printed in the USA
LVHW042102230722
724181LV00009B/410

9 781791 334826